From
Camden Passage
With Love

*The Inside Story of Camden Passage,
London's Antique Village*

From Camden Passage with love

The Inside Story of Camden Passage, London's Antique Village

John Payton

The Book Guild Ltd
Sussex England

The Book Guild Ltd
25 High Street,
Lewes, Sussex
First published 1992
© John Payton 1992
Set in Baskerville
Typeset by Kudos Graphics, Horsham
Printed in Great Britain by Antony Rowe Ltd
Chippenham, Wilts

A catalogue record for this book is
available from the British Library.

ISBN 0 86332 693 5

FOREWORD

My association with the revival of Camden Passage began soon after I had bought my first home. It was a Regency terrace house overlooking a leafy section of the Regents Canal. The house and Camden Passage were separated from one another by only a few yards. Both had fallen on hard times.

My next door neighbour, Mrs. Bonfanti, had dreamed of buying a house in the terrace when she was a young girl. She had passed by every day on her way to and from work. The owners of the houses during her youth had been prosperous professional people whose servants appeared on the front door steps every morning to polish the brass plates and door knockers. Her dream was temporarily removed from reality when she married a pastry chef.

Mr. Bonfanti eventually rose through the ranks to become the highly respected Head Chef in the kitchen of Harrods Restaurant. By that time, however, the neighbourhood had undergone a significant change. World War II had occurred. Many of the houses had been turned into supposedly temporary accommodation for families whose homes had been destroyed by the bombing of the East End of London. Meanwhile, much of Islington had become what citizens of South Kensington and Chelsea regarded as a slum.

The change in circumstances had already enabled Mrs. Bonfanti's dream to come true. It now did the same for me. I had almost despaired of being able to buy my first home. Every move in that direction had been thwarted until in 1960 there came the opportunity to buy a seedy boarding house at 2 Vincent Terrace, Islington, for £3,000. The age and state of repair of the building quickly discouraged all the normal sources of obtaining a mortgage loan, but our bank manager came to the rescue and offered a short-term loan, repayable in instalments equal to what we had previously been paying in rent. There was then nothing left to do but to ask the boarding house proprietor to give notice to his paying guests and then remove his decaying bed linen, towels and furniture from the premises. This caused him to nearly have a fit as, according to his calculations, the house was worth £1,000 and the balance had been paid for an established and profitable business.

The need for an inexpensive house had driven me to Islington, but I soon realized that I should have been guided there by commonsense. The area where I was now living was the same distance from Piccadilly Circus as was South Kensington and Chelsea, but situated in fresher air on top of a hill. The streets were wider and there seemed to be more open spaces reserved for small public parks and gardens. The depression which had temporarily settled upon the neighbourhood had served to protect beautiful Georgian and Regency buildings from demolition by property developers. There were plenty of other advantages, existing and potential, of which the majority of people seeking a London home in a sympathetic environment seemed to be totally unaware. I had already resolved to let them know what they were missing when John Payton, the initiator of Camden Passage's revival and the author of this book, first knocked on my door.

The restoration of 2 Vincent Terrace and the promotion of John Payton's development of Camden Passage occupied all of my spare time from then onwards. The promotion drew attention to the merits of living in the neighbourhood and the pleasures of visiting it for shopping. Small shops and restaurants were offering personal service in the unhurried atmosphere of an historic village within the inner city. The aim was to obtain favourable editorial publicity in the National Media at least once a week. The target was achieved because nobody who responded to the publicity was disappointed. People were grateful for being shown something interesting and exciting, of which they had previously been unaware. They recommended us to their friends and colleagues. The lesson to be learned from this became more and more apparent to me during a long career in public relations. No amount of money spent on Press contacts and advertising can sustain the sales of a bad product. Our budget was almost nil, but a good product only needs a little prompting – it very nearly sells itself.

My day to day association with Camden Passage ended after six years, as my working life required me to move from London to Sydney. The restoration of 2 Vincent Terrace had been successfully completed. The once proud building which had sunk to the depths of a gruesome lodging house had regained its pride. It was sold to Cyril Cusack, international star of stage and screen.

My knowledge of current happenings in the Camden Passage is constantly being refreshed. Truth being stranger than fiction, it will come as no surprise to learn that John Payton, author, painter, business entrepreneur and legendary saviour of the Passage, has been my neighbour in Sydney for about twenty years. We meet frequently. He successfully combines family and commercial interest at both ends of the world. At Camden Passage he remains at the helm, although his old family home is now a famous restaurant.

I hope that his book *From Camden Passage with Love* will give you as much pleasure as it has given to me.

Perry Guinness.
Formerly Publicity Project Organiser for the British Broadcasting Corporation, and now retired as Public Relations Manager in New South Wales for ICI Australia.

A self-portrait of the author, John Payton.

PREFACE

This is the previously untold story of Camden Passage – relating how it was transformed from a run-down backwater without an antique shop in sight to its present position as one of the leading art and antiques centres of the world, containing some of the finest restaurants in London. Without the community spirit and enterprise of the small shopkeepers who occupied the shops in the 1950s, this charming Georgian area would have been lost in favour of workers' flats.

In 1959, these small shopkeepers, facing diminishing business, banded together to form the Camden Passage Traders Association. Their action was closely watched by the National Press and media, who seemingly had never heard of traders working in unison and harmony and helping each other paint their shopfronts. An important by-product of Camden Passage's enterprise was the re-establishment of Islington as a fine place to live. In the early eighteenth century, Islington produced London's first developer – John Pierrepont. What he set in motion in the 1720s resulted eventually in the unique Georgian houses and Georgian and early Victorian terraces and 'squares' which made Islington a highly desirable residential area in the nineteenth century. By the 1950s most of Islington was a semi slum area, with the fine houses divided into tenements. What happened in Camden Passage in the early 60s was largely responsible for bringing back Islington to its former glory. It also started the catalyst which is now rapidly coming to fruition – of very rich developers realizing the potential of the area surrounding and in immediate proximity to Camden Passage and building their office

LONDON'S ANTIQUE VILLAGE

Camden Passage

AT THE ANGEL, ISLINGTON

This is the logo which was specially designed for
Camden Passage. It is used in all advertisements.

developments and business centres (particularly the very
fine Agricultural Hall redevelopment).

It is an inevitable product of success and importance that
the 'big boys' are moving in wherever they can secure a
foothold in Camden Passage. They, of course, have none of
the spirit that made Camden Passage great, being merely
motivated by how much money they can make out of what
was created. But no amount of money can buy the
satisfaction that obtains from creating a centre which has
brought so much joy, thrills, excitement and interest as
have the making of Camden Passage and the changing of
the face of Islington.

The writer often quotes that through the CPTA we set
the stage for a great show which would not have had the
swift, far-reaching effects that it had in the early 1960s if the
curtain had not been raised by Perry Guinness.

In the process, many fortunes were made (not the writer's
or Perry Guinness's, although they both enjoyed good
dividends) and very few lost. Small shopkeepers who had no
hope of ever escaping from their tiny businesses, except by
walking away from them, were afforded the wonderful
opportunity of selling up and making a new life, with what
to them was a lot of cash in their pockets.

10

The map on the following page will clarify the area which has come to be known as Camden Passage, although part of it is Islington High Street. Reference will be made in the text to Islington High Street (or just High Street) which forms part of the Camden Passage area and should not be confused with Upper Street, which is NOT in Camden Passage.

Number One Camden Passage is situated right opposite No. 110 Islington High Street! It then continues to number on the one side, turns the corner and heads for Upper Street, crosses the road and doubles back towards High Street until it reaches the corner. At this point, Islington High Street stops, but only after getting as far as the covered stall site. Camden Passage then takes over and continues on both sides, odd numbers to the left and even to the right, until it finally reaches Essex Road.

If you are visiting Camden Passage for the first time and arrive by tube train (Angel station), turn right outside the station and then right again at the Angel crossroads. Then you must stay with the pavement, for at the next traffic lights, Islington High Street continues on the right only and the wide main road, Upper Street, takes over. Keep to the pavement and, once you have reached The Mall on your left, you are in Camden Passage, even though you are still in the High Street.

At Phelps Cottage, the road narrows and then at the end of that block takes the sharp turn towards Upper Street, described above. Straight ahead leads you into the traffic-free part of the Georgian Camden Passage, being crossed at the halfway mark by Charlton Place, a charming history-filled row of Georgian houses, one side being built as an attractive crescent in the style of much grander houses in Regent's Park and Bath. There are two important market days for antiques and one for books, when all the stallholders are present. On those days, there are some 350 shops, boutiques and stalls to visit. Other days, except Mondays, the shops are open and buyers come from all over the world to choose from the enormous variety of antiques. It is said that there are shops to cater for everyone, from the schoolboy collector to the international dealer:

Wednesday and Saturday are the days for antiques, and

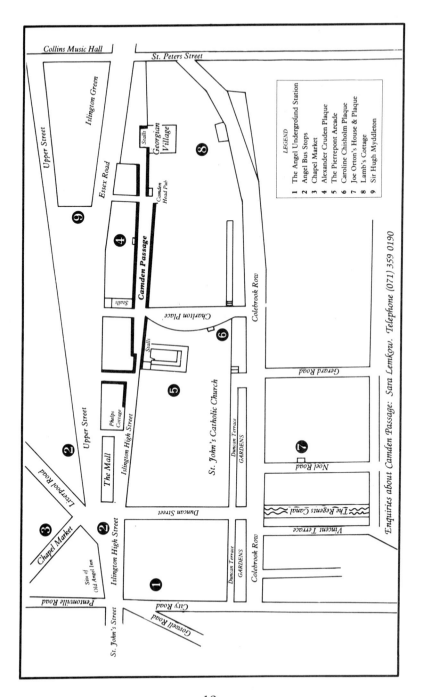

Enquiries about Camden Passage: Sara Lemkow. Telephone (071) 359 0190

LEGEND

1 The Angel Underground Station
2 Angel Bus Stops
3 Chapel Market
4 Alexander Cruden Plaque
5 The Pierrepont Arcade
6 Caroline Chisholm Plaque
7 Joe Orton's House & Plaque
8 Lamb's Cottage
9 Sir Hugh Myddleton

Thursday for books. The Wednesday market is extremely popular with dealers, who vie with each other to get there first to pick up the bargains, and this results in it starting at about 6 a.m. The other two days are more civilized.

How to get to Camden Passage:

Tube: The Angel

Buses: 4,19,30,38,73. +++++

Taxi: Just ask for Camden Passage.

1

The monotonous sound of a starter motor turning over began to interfere with my concentration, and I realized it had been going on for some time. As I looked out of the window of my music shop at 112 Islington High Street on a sunny day in 1958, Danny O'Hara got out of his new green Sunbeam Talbot 90 touring car, parked in the narrow road outside. He was looking far from happy as he raised the bonnet. Danny was a sports car fan and had just, after many years of struggle, been able to afford this expensive car and here it was, a non-starter.

The O'Hara's had come to Camden Passage in 1935 to open a toy shop at No 19, the shop that for some unknown historical reason manages to jut out into the Passage further than any other (it now houses one of the finest print shops in England). Danny O'Hara, helped by his wife, established a flourishing business which built up well until the wartime shortages forced him to use his ingenuity, when he started a small factory manufacturing dart boards. Just after the war had ended, he took the adjacent shop, No 21 Camden Passage, in addition to his exisiting shop and started to stock bicycles, and then yet another shop on the corner of Charlton Place, No 10 Camden Passage, where he sold prams. All this led him to his situation in 1958 when, having at last afforded his ultimate dream, the damn thing would not start.

There was something I had been wanting to talk about to Mr O'Hara, who was one of the few people who called me by my first name – that was the way things were in the old Camden Passage, where everyone was on polite nodding terms and certainly very few were on first-name terms with their fellow shopkeepers. I ventured out of my music shop and crossed the road to the very flustered man.

'Good morning, Mr O'Hara,' I said brightly. 'Anything I can do to help?'

'I can't get the bloody thing to go,' he moaned.

'You don't have a secret switch fitted, do you?' I asked – I had one fitted to my wife's little Mini when I bought it second-hand, and it had saved its life on many occasions. We parked her car in the road opposite the shop over which we lived (and where I had lived all my life), 112 High Street, so I had a grandstand view from an upstairs window when at night passing youths easily manipulated the lock, opened the passenger door to let in their girlfriends, leapt into the car and tried to get it going. They would be absolutely baffled when it refused to start, and would eventually have to admit defeat and leave the car, slamming the door and often kicking the tyres – all this while we quietly watched from the second floor. None of them seemed ever to suspect that there was a secret switch or, even if they had, would not have been willing to spare the time to search the car. Stealing cars is a pastime which demands a speedy getaway. When Perry Guinness had his car stolen he was required to appear in a suburban court, at great personal inconvenience, to give evidence against some youths who had been caught by the police in the act of doing a spot of burgling. One of the youths, when asked if he had anything to say in his defence, loudly and soundly condemned the poor state of maintenance of the car, much to Perry's embarrassment.

A slow smile spread across the O'Hara face, and he sheepishly went into the car and played with the switch. I began to feel like a bit of a clever-dick, but it broke down the nervousness I had felt about approaching him with an idea I had been working on for months.

He got the car started – immediately – and brightened visibly and made ready to drive off with a cheery ' Thanks'. I cleared my throat to show him that he was not going to get away that easily after my brilliant fault-finding.

'Mr O'Hara.' I started,' I have an idea I want to talk to you about. You know how the Passage has been going downhill for the past few years? Well, the time has come to either do something about it or think about moving out.'

Danny switched off the engine with obvious reluctance – now that the car was going, he wanted to hare off in it.

'You're right about business not being as good as it used to be, Johnnie,' he replied. I don't know where he got the 'Johnnie' from, I had never been called that, not even in the army - other things, but not Johnnie. 'What have you got in mind?'

'I have been saying for a couple of years that if anyone well-dressed and well-spoken comes into our shop, they must have lost their way. Look at all the scruffy, unpainted shops; look at all the shops that have been turned into little factories and have boarded-up windows; the rubbish that is dumped on that bombed site opposite your shop; look at that shop over there which belongs to the Polish gent who has let it off as a bed-sit!' I was referring to No. 11 Camden Passage, situated right on the corner of High Street and Camden Passage. It had corrugated iron roughly nailed to cover the windows. I did not know the Pole's name, having seen him only once or twice as he entered by the side door, but I had been told he was Polish by my neighbour, Mr Geere, while he was mending a puncture in my daughter's cycle for the princely sum of sixpence. 'If we don't do something about it, the whole place will come to a standstill. Well, I want to form an association of all the shopkeepers in Camden Passage so that we can get together and think about improving the place and trying to attract back some of the public. We could put some money into a kitty and start a painting scheme, and clean up some of the bombed sites and get a bit of publicity. Who knows where it could end? Do you think the shopkeepers would join me?'

'Sounds like a good idea to me,' said Danny, 'I'll go along with anything you do - you can rely on me, and I'll encourage people to join too.' With that, he hit the starter, the motor let out its throaty roar, and he sailed off in his dream car.

That bit of encouragement gave me the courage to go ahead with my plan with some hope of it being well received by the rest of the shopkeepers. It was to be a couple of years before the new Camden Passage was officially opened, and Danny O'Hara was never to see it, as he sadly died at a relatively early age. His wife carried on the business together with her daughter, Eileen, and husband John Friend, who in 1955 had left a promising career with Coventry Council and moved house and home when asked for help in running the business. This was the beginning of a long association that John Friend was to have with Camden Passage.

The problem I had spoken about to Danny was a real one, and had been getting worse over the years as the whole place became run-down. In 1919, at the end of World War 1, my father reopened the business started by his father in 1881, then in Fleet Street, and brought his young wife and one-year-old baby, my brother, to live over the shop at 112 High Street. I was born there in 1920, and this made me just the right age to be called up into the army in 1941, which occupied my life for the next five years. I was happily demobilized in 1946 and, my father having died in 1943 and my mother having developed an urge to travel the world, I took over the family music business. By 1958, I had the music shop and a very good music school with an attendance of some 300 pupils a week receiving private tuition from eight teachers. In addition, our studios were used as practice rooms, mainly by singers from the nearby Sadlers Wells Opera. Despite this, I had been noticing that fewer and fewer public were visiting Camden Passage, and the place was becoming dirtier.

In the 1920s and 30s, when enjoyment was found in the simple things of life and a happy-go-lucky evening stroll around the shops was considered to be as good an entertainment as people were likely to find or afford, Camden Passage was a bustling place, especially on Saturday evenings. The shop windows were full of interest, and there was plenty of free entertainment.

If they could afford threepence or sixpence, the Islington Empire Theatre, situated in the High Street about one hundred yards from the Angel crossroads, was putting on high drama part of the time and music hall the rest.

I remember at the age of five (1925) seeing Todd Slaughter as Sweeney Todd in 'The Demon Barber of Fleet Street'. Todd Slaughter probably knew only one or two plays, with which he and his company toured the countless music halls and theatres in the circuit throughout England.

By the time he and his company had finished the circuit and then done the rounds again with his other play, the audience had either forgotten the first one or another generation had matured.

My older brother and I had arrived very early and queued in the little alleyway, which was the entrance to 'The Gods' or the upper balcony at the side of the theatre. Time passed quickly as the buskers entertained the queue, ending each act with a collection into their cloth caps and then making way for the next turn. There were also the then inevitable peanut vendors shouting: 'Peanuts, penny-a-bag'.

When the doors opened, we paid our threepences and made a mad dash up the many flights of stairs, our peanut bag held firmly, and our hearts in our mouths in case we were overtaken, to be first there and capture a front seat in the dizzy and precarious heights of the gallery. The compulsory safety curtain was down, covered with quotations, the only one of which I recall was: 'Has this thing appeared again tonight? Macbeth', and we waited excitedly for it to rise and for the show to start, amusing ourselves by letting some peanut shells drop on to the audience in the circle seats below.

Young as I was, and accompanied by my brother who was three years older, I recall all too vividly the curtain raising to reveal the stage which simultaneously showed two levels, so that we saw Sweeney Todd's barber's shop above and the cellar below. As newly arrived midshipmen and sailors came in for a shave and haircut, their pockets brimming with money, Sweeney Todd sat them in the barber's chair (which WE could see had an identical chair upside down beneath it) and declared that he was just going to sharpen his razor. He retired to the side of the shop, made some blood-curdling cackles and a loud announcement that we could hear but the customer apparently could not or he would have taken off like a rocket, to the effect that he would 'Polish him off'. He pulled a lever rather like the one which changes the points on a railway and then revolved the chair, bringing the duplicated chair to the shop level and depositing the customer into the basement, a fall of some ten feet onto some conveniently placed spikes. Todd

19

then descended to the basement, gloating noisily as he did so, to slit the victim's throat. This sort of activity scared the life out of this five-year-old and, when the interval thankfully came, I told my brother that I was 'off' and ran the 200 yards home as fast as I could.

The pavements were full of people in the gaslit street, and I had to run in the road to reach the safety of my parents in the busy music shop as soon as ever possible. When my brother finally returned, he said he had wondered what had happened to me - he had not even heard me say that I was going. He said that it was explained at the end of the play that the men who played the part of Sweeney Todd's victims had metal plates attached to their backs under their clothing, so that they did not hurt themselves! How they found 'actors' to risk being propelled from an upside-down chair on to their backs on the floor some ten foot below is hard to imagine, metal plates or no metal plates, rubber spikes or not.

But it was not necessary to fork out threepences to be entertained.

Behind the old power station which provided power for the tramway system (now The Mall), where the road widens out in front of Phelps Cottage, was a favourite place for street performers of all types. A very good Punch & Judy show was often set up there by a Mr Carcass, a Gypsy, who lived over No. 110 High Street for a few years in the mid 20s. He was a rough character, and occupied the rooms over the shop with his wife. They spent much of their time in the pub (now Frederick's Restaurant at No. 106) and kept a hedgehog as a pet. This animal had a party trick which it seemed to enjoy immensely – Mr Carcass turned it onto its back and poured beer into the well it formed, and it sucked up the beer as fast as Carcass could tip it in.

When Carcass himself was well and truly drunk, screams would come from his rooms as he beat his wife, who was not incapable of doing a bit of beating back on her own account. As a child, I thought it was Punch beating Judy, so it did not matter too much.

There was another married couple who lived in the murky basement of 110 High Street in the early 1930s and they were responsible for some fine melodrama *without* first getting sozzled. They had the wife's sister living with them, and it seemed that she did not exactly get on with her brother-in-law, for now and then, following a loud altercation he would chase her, she screaming loudly, into the garden at the rear, brandishing a large kitchen knife. I witnessed one of these performances. She fell to the ground, and he kneeled over her with a knife held high.

'Imelda!' she screamed.

'Yes, Freda,' came a calm reply from the basement where they lived.

'He's *killing* me,' Freda screeched.

'Yes, Freda,' came the quiet response.

'Imelda – *save* me – I am being *murdered*' pleaded Freda, apparently beside herself with anguish.

'Oh! Yes, Freda.' was the best Imelda could manage by way of interest. And so it went on. Nobody was ever killed as far as I know, but it was good entertainment.

Another performer behind the power station, whom I saw only once, was a lady who stood upon a pedestal of some sort while her sponsor declared to the interested spectators that she was the only lady in the world who could turn her body at the waist so that she ended up with her feet facing north while her face and upper parts took a look at the southern aspect. But before she could be persuaded to carry out this dangerous manoeuvre a collection would be necessary, so he went round with a hat, getting rid of half his audience in the process (but many came back when he had gone past). Having collected, he counted out the takings and then repeated his claim about his companion's extraordinary abilities as far as twisting herself went. But, he had to say, she could not do it for the paltry amount he had collected but, just to show good faith, she would get herself started on the act. The pedestalled lady then began to swing to the right and left, but seemed to agree with her friend about the 'takings' and was reluctant to demonstrate her full skills until enough pennies were in the hat. She kept this swinging up while her friend (hopefully her friend) continued his patter and made a further couple of collections. As I had been sent out by my parents on an errand and they were awaiting my return, which should have happened some half-an-hour before, I reluctantly had to leave them to get on with it, not that I was really entitled to see such a phenomenon, having not contributed in any way to the collections. I have often wondered how the show ended, but I bet it was not with the lady facing in two directions at the same time.

Another performer was the escapologist who, stripped to the waist, was noisily but securely tied up in chains by his colleague, with the help of a witness from the audience who tested and testified, between the inevitable collections, that the chains were indeed biting into flesh. Once a further collection was pronounced to be satisfactory, the chained prisoner would then do his stuff, hurling himself around on the road, gasping, panting and sweating at the impossible task, but amazingly slowly loosening the chains as he relaxed his muscles.

The organ-grinders were frequently in evidence, and these gentlemen lasted well into the 1950s. They hired their machine from an old Italian by the name of Tomasso, who lived in nearby Elia Street, Islington, just near the Regents Canal at Duncan Terrace. Tomasso kept his machines in a shed which was also his workshop. When Tomasso died, there was no successor to carry on what was quite an art. Tomasso made these 'barrel organs' and, surprisingly, used to buy the sheet music from us ('I can do any tune in my organs', he boasted in his Italian accent). His skill involved inserting metal pins into a large wooden cylinder, judging both the position and the timing to get it to activate the correct steel note at the right moment. The sound produced is unique and is reminiscent of old London, gaslamps and fish and chips in newspaper.

One of these organ-grinders, Arthur, of whom we became quite fond – a thin, scruffy down-and-out Scot – played his barrel-organ with great dignity, standing proudly and upright at the side of the organ, timing the turning of the handle, he thought, with great musical skill, such as would be expected of Sir Thomas Beecham. He seemed to think that, as a music shop, we were entitled to special privileges, and he would park his barrel organ outside the shop and give a special performance, looking to us for approval which we never failed to give. A downpour of rain never put him off for a moment. One day he turned up and the rain was absolutely teeming down, but Arthur operated on the show-biz principal that 'The Show must go on', and he gave his concert standing there with a proud and musically important look mixed with a blissful smile on his face, chin held high. He was absolutely soaked but at the end of his repertoire, he came into the shop for the praise and sixpence which we always gave, leaving large puddles to be cleaned up as soon as he moved to his next pitch. (I wonder what Tomasso thought when the sodden instrument was returned at the end of the day?) He was a down-and-out but liked it that way. His father owned a cinema in Glasgow, he told us, and would have bailed him out any time, but he was happy the way he was.

Arthur at one time recruited an equally scruffy companion – a tall, thin man who had no confidence at all in himself, and who played the violin quite well. He accompanied the barrel organ, with Arthur, as the leader of the duo, setting the pace by the speed of turning the handle, allowing himslf a small conducting motion now and then to ensure that his employee was kept in order. The violinist could never muster the courage to come into the shop when he wanted a new string for his violin, but sent his Scottish maestro in while he himself hovered nervously and uncertainly outside, peering in at the window but quickly turning away if we looked in his direction. One day he was not on duty when our friend came to serenade us, and Arthur told us that a well-known band-leader had heard him play and offered him a place in his band! His benefactor may have been the famous bandleader Geraldo (Gerald Bright), who lived in Duncan Terrace!

Someone else used to hover outside our music shop, peeping in to see if there was a customer and waiting outside if there was, until the coast was clear. This was a spiritualist who operated from the first floor of the house at 90 High Street. He had a driving mirror fixed up outside the window on the first floor, presumably because he wished to know who was knocking at the door and his spiritual contacts were not to be relied upon to provide that information. Once he got into our shop, he would buy, as quickly and furtively as possible, plastic trumpets, and we assumed that these, once the lights were dimmed, were somehow persuaded to float around the room.

In those 1920s and 30s in Camden Passage, there was a shop (which is now part of 'Becks') that sold day-old chicks. Hundreds of them thrived in the shop window which was heated by an electric bulb. There were also two umbrella shops (related to each other, but deadly enemies) flourishing; two hat shops owned by the same firm 'Brewers'; and two sweet shops – one was rather 'posh', with sweets priced at three ounces for tuppence, whereas the other managed to dispense two ounces for one penny. On Saturday evenings, on the wide pavement at the Essex Road end of the Passage, a seafood stall, brightly lit by an acetylene lamp, dispensed cockles, mussels, whelks, winkles and oysters – on saucers if you wished to eat them there, or in newspaper if not. Right next to the 'whelk stall' was a man who had an enormous set of brass scales, supported by an A-frame. He would guess your weight, having first felt his customer in various places – greeted with much giggling by young ladies – before putting on shining brass weights to check his skilled assessment. If he was right, you paid. You mostly paid. . . .

Just across the road, another attraction was the famous Collins Music Hall which was situated on the built-up side of the Islington Green triangle. Charlie Chaplin, in the early 1900s, appeared there when just a boy, and is reputed to have been taken to the local toy shop by Kate Carney. (The toy shop, situated at the Essex Road entrance to Camden Passage, was still there until the early 60s.) There is still a plaque to show where Collins Music Hall was until, also in the early 1960s, it suffered from a disastrous and most spectacular fire which took place in Anderson's wood yard next to it, and this closed its doors (already half-closed anyway, even though the old music-hall comedian Lew Lake and his brother Len did their best to revive it in the 1950s).

Lew Lake ran Collins Music Hall, mainly from the bar at the back of the auditorium. This bar was at the entrance to the theatre and at the back of the audience. It had walls covered with signed photographs of music hall stars and celebrities. It was possible to keep an eye on the stage from the bar, so, with the aid of the special stock of Lew's special taste in beer under the counter, this was where the management took place.

Lew's brother, Len Lake, however, specialized in 'talking effigies' which he invented, made and tested in a large hall on the first floor directly over the music hall. After visiting my recording studio (to glorify one of my activities), he made a spoken recording onto a waxed disc and then invited me to attend a private demonstration of his creations in his workshops. I went one evening and met him in the bar, where he said we must remain until he and his brother had watched what he described as the most fantastic turn ever to appear on the music hall stage. With his brother coming in every five minutes or so to demolish one of his private bottles of beer and then going off to oversee the music hall, I stood with Len in the bar, whiling away the time until this fantastic act was to appear on stage. Lew came in to warn us that this earth-shattering event was now about to occur, and we went to the back of the theatre. The turn came on and both Lew and Len completely ignored it – took no notice at all – but carried on talking with their backs facing the stage. (I did not think much of it either!)

Len took me upstairs to his workshop. With the performer's sense of the dramatic, there was just one bare bulb burning, hanging from a twisted cable and creating eerie shadows throughout the murky hall. He sat me on a spindly chair right under the light while he went off to manipulate his controls, explaining his every action in a voice, the tone of which would have done justice to a performance of *King Lear*, the sound of the music hall beneath as a constant background. Suddenly, out of the shadows, apparently activated by the recording I had made, a very large bottle of Bovril started to talk to me, extolling the merits of its contents; then an Oxo Cube, followed by a man-sized beer bottle – all of which had a moving mouth attached. Then came what Len thought was his *pièce de résistance* – 'Talking Billy Beacon', a traffic crossing beacon – the amber globe of which had eyes, nose and a mouth that moved and which, Len explained, he took to schools and got it to tell the children how to be careful crossing the road. Not a bad idea at that.

25

A fish and chip shop flourished in Camden Passage, just near the Camden Head pub, but the premises were demolished in the early 1960s with other shop premises by the uncooperative and unimaginative Islington Council at a time when it was obvious that more shops were desperately needed. Ignoring our pleas to have shop premises on the street level and build their beloved council flats above, they rapidly demolished the premises and erected flats.

The public houses – Camden Head, the Shakespeare, the Duke of Sussex (where now stands the famous Fredericks' restaurant) and the York did brisk business in those pre-war days. The Camden Head still has some unique fine cut glass windows looking on to the Passage and retains the atmosphere of a Victorian London pub.

Where the stalls are situated at 122 Islington High Street, in front of the Pierrepont Arcade, there was a wet fish shop which was still in existence until one of Hitler's incendiary bombs put an end to its career in 1943. In 1830 it was a butcher's shop.

At 14 Camden Passage in the 20s and 30s, a bowler-hatted Mr Phillips might be seen standing outside his second-hand and odds-and-ends shop, displaying a very prominent belly under a waistcoat complete with silver watch chain, his marvellous specimen of a beautifully ugly bandy white bulldog at his side; that is, until the police periodically took them both away for a spell 'inside' for receiving stolen property. They would both reappear some months later, Mr Phillips' belly gone due to the frugal prison diet, but with the bulldog in as good shape as ever. It was assumed that there was an institution for dogs, and we always hoped it was not behind bars, like his master was fated to be.

In the 1920s and 30s number 6 Camden Passage was occupied by 'Thomas's the Printers', whose window was full of sample visiting cards and wedding invitations. But every now and then, a Black Maria would screech to a halt at the narrow entrance to the Passage, while another arrived at Charlton Place. Both disgorged policemen who raced into the premises, arrested everyone therein and emerged, escorting the captives into the Black Marias. It seems that the printing was only a 'front', and that the main living came from bookmaking – illegal, of course. It was hard luck for anyone who had gone in for a friendly chat, as happened to the dignified crippled lady from the umbrella shop at No.8, who never really lived down being dragged protesting into the Black Maria and thence to the local police station, no doubt to the intense satisfaction of the other umbrella shopkeeper. The lady in question would, given the slightest opportunity, pass on a message from 'the other side', rather fancying herself as a spiritualist. But she did not get the message that the cops were coming. . . .

It seemed to me in the 1930s that people may have been poor, but they had the ability to enjoy themselves with the simple things of life, with a seemingly contented mind. A walk through Camden Passage on Saturday evening was one of their enjoyments, and probably provided as much or more pleasure to them then as does a night in front of the television now.

However, by the 1950s, due to the upheaval of the war, there was no doubt that habits had changed and, as a consequence, pedestrian traffic dwindled and there was not the demand for shops in Camden Passage. Many shopkeepers had moved away or been called into the army or just plain gone broke during the war. Those that remained were facing an increasing struggle as the public numbers diminished, perhaps because television was gaining the attention of those who previously went out for a stroll around. If the Passage was to survive, something drastic had to be done.

In 1955, the shop next door to my music shop (No.110 High St) had become vacant, having for some years been occupied by one Mr. Fusco, a second-hand dealer who was whispered to be one of the biggest 'fences' (receiver of stolen property) in the area. Fusco, a short, stocky, swarthy little man with enormous nervous energy, took over the shop during the war at a time when firstly bombs and incendiaries and then doodle-bugs (Hitler's V1s) were raining down on London by day and night. He had a blonde wife who had the most startlingly beautiful blue eyes that you could ever wish to see, and a family of six children ranging in ages from two to fifteen. My then recently widowed mother was alone in 112 (the music shop), and

Fusco made frequent declarations to her that, in return for the kindness she showed to his family – for when they arrived they did not have any bedding or clothing, and she set them up for the sake of the children – if a bomb fell on her premises, as seemed highly likely at a time when bombs and incendiaries fell on London like confetti, he would dig her out with his own bare hands. Fortunately, the sincerity of his declaration was never put to the test.

It must be admitted that there was never a dull moment during the Fusco years, with constant police raids and strange happenings during the night. I was told by a 'reliable source' that on one of the raids, the police lined him up with his family in descending order while they searched the shop. From beneath the counter the police produced some lovely jewellery (I like to think it was a tiara).

'What about this?' asked the cops.

'Ooo bought that?' countered Fusco, glaring at his children. The youngest, a sweet little girl then about four years old, admitted that she had!

He was a kind man, and quickly volunteered one day to take me to pick up a large over-mantle gilded mirror I had bought in a shop a couple of miles away. Fusco had acquired a high-powered, long bonneted vehicle with a V8 engine which had served as an ambulance during the war. He told me to jump in. His assistant, a diminutive creature called Arthur, jumped in too, and sat perched on the back of the driver's seat like a monkey. It very quickly became obvious that Fusco's driving expertise, judged on a scale of 1 to 10, was Nil. We careered along Essex Road at a very high speed, mainly on the wrong side of the road, forcing several cars to mount the pavement to avoid elimination. After what seemed a lifetime, we screamed to a halt outside the shop where I had bought the large mirror, heaved it in the back of the ambulance where Arthur was told to look after it. We took off at 'smash & grab' speed towards home, via Highbury New Park. The consequence of taking a sharp corner at thrice the sensible speed resulted in the mirror crashing on to its back and the glass shattering into a thousand pieces. Without any hesitation, Fusco skidded to a halt in the middle of the road, leapt out, he and Arthur grabbed the mirror and shook all the broken glass on to the middle of the road, leaving only the frame and backing board which they threw back into the van, jumped back in and continued the journey as if nothing untoward had happened (I think a few untoward things might have happened to the tyres of any following vehicles). I can tell you that something untoward had jolly nearly happened to me! I was so grateful to get back to Camden Passage in one piece that I thanked him profusely for his kindness, and made a resolution never to accept any future favours.

Some weeks later, Fusco offered me some advice on the maintenance of my car. He told me that his ambulance had suddenly come to a complete standstill, and the mechanic he called in told him that the engine had seized up due to the absence of oil and water. 'No-one told me that you had to put anything in except petrol!' said Fusco. I believe that.

When, in 1955, Fusco and his family left to go to South Africa, it was a relief to both myself and to the local constabulary, who had mounted a constant roster of plainclothes police to watch the shop. Rather than risk a similar tenant taking over, I took the lease and opened an artists' materials and picture-framing shop, putting a manager in charge. Not surprisingly, this shop lost money consistently for many years, but it paid off in other ways, as we shall see.

A shop which was very important to the scheme of improvement I had in mind was No.100, Islington High Street. This shop faced the main road from its position between The Mall and Phelps Cottage, and could be seen from the high pavement in Upper Street, which was then quite a busy shopping area. Clearly, if this shop looked interesting, people might bother to cross the road and visit Camden Passage. But it did not look good – in fact it looked awful. It was occupied by a wholesaler of hardware items who had no interest at all in making the premises look clean and inviting. In order to get into his premises when he arrived in the morning, he had to bring out on to the pavement a number of dustbins and other large items which he had for sale, and these stayed there all day until closing time. They were often accompanied by an amount of straw and newspapers, and these worked their way along Camden Passage on the breeze, making the place look terribly untidy. The shop was being used as a warehouse, and looked that way.

My chance came when, in 1958, this wholesaler moved out to larger premises, and a 'To Let' sign went up, put there by estate agents, Cyril Leonard & Co., whose premises were in Pentonville Road, just around the corner at the Angel crossroads. I immediately went to see the manager, a very nice, understanding man, and told him of my ideas for the improvement of Camden Passage. I begged him not to let the shop to another dustbin merchant, but to try to get a quality tenant. He called to see me quite often and told me of the various applications he had received and turned down – potentially sleazy cafés, a secondhand clothes merchant, fancy goods wholesalers and other businesses whch would be unsuitable if we were to improve our image. He kept those premises empty for many months until one day he came to see me, beaming all over his face.

'I've got it!' he said, 'I've just let No.100 to an antique dealer, and quite a good one at that!'

In due course, an ex-actor turned antique dealer, Leigh Underhill, with artist companion Frank Stanton, came along, redecorated the shop beautifully and moved in to live in the upstairs flat. They are still there, and have the honour to be Camden Passage's first antique dealers. What a victory that was. Leigh later told me that when he came to view the shop, he looked along the High Street and saw the art shop and thought 'If he can make a living, so can I.' Little did he know . . .

Another advancement came when the tenant of 108 High Street agreed to cooperate in a small way. The premises belonged to Harry Bailey, who made popular light-weight racing cycles under the well-known brand name 'Macleans Featherweight Cycles'. He had retail shop premises in the Upper Street in an arcade of shops at the bus-stop. The bus-stop is still there, but the arcade has long gone, as have the underground public toilets which were there, never to be replaced. He used the High Street premises as a factory and, because he had no use for the shop window, he had a large plank of wood nailed diagonally across it for security. Harry was not the most generous of men, no doubt due to the struggle to exist and keep a family in his earlier years, so when I approached him and told him what I was doing and I asked him if he would please smarten up the factory front, he amazed me by not only agreeing, but excelled himself by having the plank of wood removed, the shopfront painted, having his name signwritten on the facia and putting one of his cycles in the window! This cycle provided one of the funniest incidents I have ever seen.

One of the enterprising local youths, of which there were plenty at that time, chose the hour of midnight to hurl a brick through Harry Bailey's window. We slept on the top floor of 112 High Street, facing the street. I leapt out of bed and witnessed this youth bringing his prize to the middle of the road. He jumped on it and started making his getaway at what would have been at least 60 miles per hour at the rate he was pedalling. I say 'would have been', because he had not bargained on Harry's reluctance to provide free cycles for the locals, or anyone else, for that matter. The cycle was so geared that when our friend cycled at 60 mph, a true speed of about 1 mph resulted. There was this youth pedalling like fury and moving like a snail and being unable to find the time to think why this should be so, he being in a desperate hurry to put as much distance as possible, in the shortest possible time, between himself and Camden Passage.

A London Bobby appeared round the corner by Phelps Cottage and, at an easy lope, caught up with the racing cyclist as he was steering his way towards Upper Street but not getting there. The cop pushed the youth off the bike, at which time I thought it might be of some help if I went to give a hand, preferably with a pair of trousers on and a jacket over my pyjamas on that cold night.

The cop was summoning a Black Maria from a telephone booth on the far side of Upper Street when I arrived. He had the youth with his nose touching the rear wall of the telephone box, one arm well up behind his back. Once the call was finished, he brought the youth very rapidly out of the telephone box with a sharp tug which had him reeling along the pavement.

'Try to escape, would you?' asked the cop, who promptly leapt on his captive and gave him a thump or two. Very soon the Black Maria arrived and carted its prisoner away, and the cop turned to me.

'Thanks for your help,' he said. 'I hope you don't think I was too rough, but the truth is that he'll be in front of a magistrate tomorrow, and as like as not he will be warned that he must not do this sort of thing again, and sent home. I think that this one will not pinch any more bicycles.'

I think he was right about that! My music shop window had been broken so many times by aspiring local musicians who helped themselves to guitars and piano accordions or whatever was in fashion at the time, that I was glad to see one of them discouraged from this practice. It became so bad in the Beatlemania era that I had to get some sturdy lift gates fitted, secured by a massive padlock.

2

In 1959, I typed up a letter of which I made a number of copies on my Remington duplicator (one of those that required a stencil, ink and a roller), addressed to the shopkeepers of Camden Passage and Islington High Street, in which I outlined the general idea of the scheme and invited them to attend a meeting and to join The Camden Passage Traders' Association (CPTA). This meeting was to take place in my art shop – the only place big enough to hold a meeting – and I asked them to bring their own chair. The notice set out the basic aims of the Association, which were, firstly, to devise a painting scheme designed to create a pleasing result; to try to get some of the closed shops open, and to think of ways to clean up the bombed site at 122 High Street and the empty site at 29 Camden Passage, where a dangerous structure had been pulled down. Both sites had become a dumping ground by a lot of locals, and it was not uncommon to find an old mattress, a couple of old tyres, cardboard boxes and newspapers dumped on them (these being amongst the more mentionable deposits). The local council was fed up with being called upon to come and remove the garbage, and we were fed up with seeing it.

The meeting was surprisingly well attended, and the following is a list of trades represented:

Two newsagents/tobacconists.

Undertaker (trading under a name that sounded more like a battleship than an undertaker – H.M. Repuke).

Two printers (both using their shops as factories).

Gramophone record/sewing machine shopkeeper Harry Levey, of whom more later.

Shoe repairer or cobbler from one of those minute shops

at the top of Charlton Place.

Toys, cycle and pram shop (O'Hara's).

Electrical/toys (Becks).

Upholsterer (another closed shop). David Smith, also of whom more later.

Grocer (Fred Slapp aided by his wife, at No.4 Camden Passage, had reigned supreme over the local housewives, as did most grocers during the shortages of the war years, sometimes but not often allowing a little extra on top of the ration coupons. His shoulder of bacon was kept on one of the stairs at the back of the shop, which led up to his small flat. His Alsation dog found that a comfortable place to rest, and was often fast asleep on it! However, it did not mind being disturbed if someone wanted some bacon).

Builders' merchant, Lewis Williams. (Where now stands the Gateway Arcade).

Secondhand clothing dealer, 'Lou's'.

Cycle repairer/gramophone records, Alf Geere (puncture repairer at sixpence a time).

Ladies' lingerie (sadly run-down now that the wartime black market was over – Mr Lewis at 120 High Street could supply silk stockings without any clothing coupons throughout the war!).

Publican.

Music shop/school (mine).

Paint & wallpaper retailer.

and one antique dealer (Leigh Underhill).

The meeting was a lively affair, and reflected the desperation being felt through the steadily declining trade. In no time at all it was agreed that a painting scheme would be welcome (but it was not clear how we could obtain one), and that it would be a good idea to concrete over the offensive sites at 122 High Street and 29 Camden Passage, behind the Shakespeare public house. How this was to be achieved nobody had the slightest idea, firstly because it would be essential to trace the owner of the 122 site (we knew that the Courage brewery owned 29 Camden Passage), and get permission to improve them, and secondly because we did not have a clue between us how to go about concreting! However, we agreed to make enquiries in order to establish a likely cost by the next meeting.

My suggestion that every shop should donate two shillings and sixpence per week into a fund was also adopted, and I volunteered to become the collector and treasurer (a thankless task which was to lead to some funny situations). It was during this meeting that I declared that we would turn our Camden Passage into one of the leading streets of London – a remark which I thought was a trifle over-optimistic.

The meeting then addressed the question of what to do with the sites, if and when they were concreted. Leigh Underhill, our newly-arrived antique dealer, said that perhaps we should try to establish a small antique stalls market, and this met with general approval.

A few letters sent to paint manufacturers brought an offer from one. They said they would send their designer along to have a look at Camden Passage and draw up a painting plan, it being understood that we would recommend their particular brand of paint, which they were prepared to supply at half-price. We accepted with alacrity, and a very charming lady came along to take a look around. A few weeks later, she presented a beautifully-drawn plan of the whole Passage, suitably coloured in various well-thought-out blending shades. This was displayed at the second meeting of the CPTA, and received universal approval. As to the empty site at 122, I had located the owner, our local doctor, and had his agreement to grant a lease to whoever was going to occupy the site. A couple of members had some estimates for concreting, and these were met with horror, as our funds would not run to it. We decided that we should try to find out how to do the job ourselves as a community effort, and report to the next meeting.

I followed up the painting scheme by asking the designer to revisit the Passage, and offered to escort her to each of the premises in turn to discuss their paint requirements. I came to wish I had not done so. Almost every member we visited said that he thought the scheme a good one for the Passage, but not for him personally ! 'I've always been dark brown and cream,' said one, 'and that's what I'm sticking to . . . and I've got my own paint.' Another had jumped the gun and painted his shop bright orange. The upholsterer stated that he had no intention of painting at all. When I suggested that we would be happy as a team to paint his shop for him at absolutely no cost to him, he said that he would put some unthinkable substance on his windows if anyone dared to touch his shop. One after another came up with a refusal, and I was devastated and terribly embarrassed. At the end of the day, we had to admit defeat, and I thought the good lady was very charming about the whole thing. Only two of us bought some paint, and it was in the planned colours.

But some good came out of it – not to the paint manufacturer, but to Camden Passage – because people who had never considered painting their shops – one had a shopfront that had not been painted for at least twenty-five years – now gave them coats of paint, albeit in various unacceptable shades.

At the next meeting of our Association, we were joined by two new antique dealers, both as a result of Leigh Underhill's initiative. The first was Arnold Cawthrow, a journalist who wrote a childrens' column in a national paper under the name of 'Big Chief I-Spy'. He owned a full set of Indian Chief's feathers to prove it, and published some very instructive books under the 'I-Spy' title. This column inspired children to chase all over London seeking out various interesting items – hence the I-Spy. Arnold moved into No.16 Camden Passage, and I must remember to tell of the day when the Queen Mother visited Camden Passage and went to his shop, but that was later.

The other antique dealer was Guy des Rochers, a French-Canadian model. Guy was a well-known face, having appeared in nationwide advertisements for a famous brand of cigarettes. He came to me and asked if I could find him premises as he desperately wanted to become an antique dealer. I was able to persuade Mr Lewis, the run-down ladies' underwear shopkeeper of black-market silk-stocking fame at 120 High Street, to let the shop, for which he charged the princely rent of twenty-five shillings per week. As he was paying only fifteen shillings a week for the whole premises and lived upstairs with his family, he was delighted with the arrangement, and so was Guy who, incidentally, never looked back and became a very high-class dealer. Guy made it clear to me at our first meeting that he was a 'woman-hater'. I was not too sure what he meant, but had a vague suspicion. Nowadays he would have told me that he was 'gay', as would a lot of other antique dealers who came to Camden Passage if the law had then permitted them.

When the question of concreting the site of 122 was again raised, we had one in our midst who had some know-how in that direction. Frank, Guy's Irish companion, had experience of roadworks and was able to give some expert advice. This gave us the courage to plan to get some formwork, some metal and to order some ready-mixed concrete, and for as many of us as possible to congregate on the site in our worst clothes on the Sunday morning to do some navvying. In the first session, about eight members turned up to work and a few more to watch. We did roughly one half of the site, and what hard work it was for us laymen, leaving us tottering about for several days. A similar session the following week was not at all well attended by workers (the Irish ex roadworker being notable by his absence), but the watchers kept an eye on us. This proved to be an even worse back-breaking experience for those who did turn up, but the job was completed.

Now we had to think about the market-stalls idea. First we would need some tables and canopies. A few enquiries elicited the information that the cost of these items, plus the cost of concreting 29 Camden Passage (we could not face doing it ourselves after the first effort) was substantial enough to be beyond the means of the meagre funds in hand from the two-and-sixpence a week subscriptions. What was also becoming quite clear to me was that many of those 2/6d subscribers were stretched to their limit – 'Come back next week', another form of 'Mother says she's out!', some would say when I presented myself for their half-crowns! Any suggestion of a substantial increase could trigger, perhaps if not a riot, some hard feelings.

The sum required for the stalls and canopies was not an awful lot. I wanted everyone in Camden Passage, rather than any one person, to be able to benefit from anything that took place, so I formed a Company with enough £1 shares to cover the cost of the stalls and canopies. I sent an offer to all members of the CPTA inviting them to take up

£10-worth of shares for each shop. Many would have nothing to do with such an enterprise, but I raised enough to go ahead with the purchase of the tables and canopies and to get 29 Camden Passage concreted by a small local contractor. Thus, Camden Passage Sites Ltd was launched, a company which still exists and thrives today, paying very healthy dividends to those intrepid shopkeepers, and their descendants, who risked buying their £10's-worth of shares. A few have now retired, and regard the income from their wise investment as part of their pension.

Some advertisements soon brought forth a number of takers for the stalls, and in no time a bustling market was established on Saturdays. Some, but not many, of those first stallholders in 1960 are still with the market today. Others are now very successful antique dealers.

By the time June 1960 arrived, we felt we were getting things together. I thought I would visit the Town Hall to see what help and encouragement they might like to give to our enterprise, which was obviously going to do a lot of good to the Borough of Islington.

It would have been reasonable to expect that Islington Borough Council would have been delighted at what we were doing and anxious to give all the help they could. Far from it – I found that we seemed to be not at all popular in the Town Hall. I wrote many letters and had interviews with the Town Clerk and the Borough Engineer, both of whom were singularly unhelpful.

I wanted some small signs to be put on lamp-posts near the Angel Tube, to show visitors the way to Camden Passage.

'Can't be done,' said the Borough Engineer.

'Why not?' I asked.

'We do not have to give a reason,' was the reply.

I would have remained puzzled by the attitude of the Council had not a couple of events taken place.

Our music shop had as a customer a young man who was a very good guitarist and folk singer. As an occupation, entertaining had proved too precarious, and he had taken a job at the Town Hall to tide him over until he could become better established in the entertainment world. Even at this distance of time it would be best if I did not mention a name but, for the sake of this story, I will call him Paul. He has since become well-known and successful in the entertainment world. I used to tell Paul what was happening in Camden Passage, and he was extremely interested, enthusiastic and sympathetic. One day, after I had returned from a battle at the Town Hall and had been made a vague promise to consider one of my requests for some improvements for Camden Passage, in came Paul.

'You think they are going to do something about it, don't you?' he asked. 'Well, you've another think coming. They have no intention of doing anything for you – I heard what they had to say when you left.'

Great! I had a self-appointed 'mole' at the Town Hall, completely free of charge! In the months to come, I was kept aware of what was *really* going on.

The reason for the lack of cooperation became clear during a visit which I made to the Borough Engineer's office with a scheme to preserve the existing old gas lamp-posts and to have them converted to electricity at our own cost. We were concerned that Camden Passage would be caught up in the scheme then in progress to take out the charming Victorian gaslamps and replace them with concrete posts with soda lights – a perfectly good and progressive scheme for the dark backstreets of Islington, but not for Camden Passage.

'Cannot be done,' said the Borough Engineer.

Well, of course, it could be done and has been done many times elsewhere. No amount of arguments would change his mind. The streets were being converted to new lamps. I found I had to refuse to take 'No' for an answer, and just sat there and insisted. The BE called in various members of his staff to back him up, and also called for a large map which was mounted on cardboard and which was about the size of the top of his desk. After some more stubborn insistence from me, I was asked by the BE to excuse them for a few moments. They all retired to a far corner of the large office and conferred in whispers! I got up and had a look at the map, and quickly saw that a large part of Camden Passage seemed to be included in a demolition scheme, to be replaced by workers' flats and houses. The BE looked round saw me perusing his map and nearly had a fit.

'You can't look at that!' he shouted. Too late, I had. A

Georgian gem was nearly lost for all times. What we were doing had caused all the shop values to increase dramatically, and I assume that this upset the budget the Council had for the compulsory requisition of properties in Camden Passage.

As a result of my visit, things started to happen in the lamp-post business. The normal system was that a team of workmen would turn up and put in the new concrete lamps next to the old gas lamp-posts. Some weeks later, these lamps would be connected to electricity and then, after a further lapse of time, another team would come and remove the gaslamps (these were supposed to be made available for purchase by the public, but they seemed to disappear and be unavailable when enquiries were made. Some malicious soul in the know told me they ended up at a council official's home for later sale at much more than the £1 at which they were supposed to be available to the public). The whole process of replacement normally took many weeks. but in our case a team of workmen swooped on Camden Passage, erected the concrete lamps, connected them and removed the gaslamps *all in one day*. We were all furious. As luck would have it, the then Mayor of Islington walked past my shop while all this was going on, and I ran out and intercepted him and told him that it was a disgrace. He quite agreed, but was powerless to do anything.

The Town Clerk at this time and for many years before, was one H. Dixon Clark. It was to him that I had to direct a number of requests and in each case, was frustrated. Again I had the strong feeling that we were being discouraged at every turn. Eventually, after many unsuccessful written requests, I asked for and was granted a meeting with him to discuss matters. Dixon Clark, I found, was an opulent-. looking overweight person with a loud and terribly affected style of speaking – a grotesque bogus Oxford accent, it could be called, delivered in a very slow drawl. I also found that he had a disconcerting habit of puffing clouds of smoke between himself and myself, and wondered whether it was supposed to stop me seeing his eyes. There was no need for this manoeuvre, as his bushy eyebrows carried out that task very well. His office had a large desk, and I was directed to a chair at one corner of it, whilst his assistant sat at the other corner. Behind a pretence of being most interested and helpful, he blocked everything I asked for, using his side-kick to confirm his reasons. This had been going on for a little while when a telephone call came through to Dixon Clark's phone. He had a short conversation in his affected drawl, then asked whoever it was to hold on while he 'had a think about it'. He covered the mouthpiece: 'Quick,' he hissed to his assistant (no casual drawl or any sign of Oxford now), 'Look up No.6 So & So Street. They say we haven't given them the planning approval we promised!' It was obviously very serious.

The assistant rushed over to a file at the other side of the office, went through it and found the file in question. Clark grabbed it and rapidly perused it.

'Damn!' he said. He lifted his hand from the mouthpiece. The natural voice was gone and the drawl came back: 'Helloooo – now I remember -' he drawled and continued with a lot of 'high class' talk I did not bother to listen to.

I got nowhere with my requests, and this was the last time he was 'in' when I asked to be connected to him. On a couple of occasions when I was particularly concerned and had been told that he was out, my 'mole' told me he was in and at what time he went out to lunch. I turned up at the Town Hall and waited for him to come down on his way to lunch and waylaid him. He did not seem to be very pleased about that.

It was a couple of years later that a reporter from the *Evening Standard* called to see me. He said he was sure that the Council had done nothing to help Camden Passage, and asked if that was correct. I confirmed this. He said he had been along to the opening of the Dagmar Puppet Theatre in Dagmar Terrace, and all the Councillors he had spoken to had told him how they had made Camden Passage what it then was!

In 1964, the Islington Council published a guide to Islington. It made no mention at all of Camden Passage. When questioned about this by the press, Dixon Clark said: 'No comment.'

I was receiving enquiries from plenty of interested antique dealers and would-be antique dealers, for shops and stalls. If a shop became vacant, it was snapped up immediately.

Because a lot of the stallholders were amateurs, just trying their hand and therefore very inexperienced, there were plenty of bargains around, and the word was spreading amongst antique traders that they had better arrive early on Saturday mornings if they wanted to be 'in' on these bargains. Very often, a crowd would assemble at a newcomer's stall and watch him unwrap his goods. Each item would be grabbed and held by a dealer, and very often the stallholder would be left with almost nothing to display, having sold his stock in a few minutes. I remember one middle-aged man who asked to hire a stall to see how he would fare as an antique dealer. He explained that he had collected early English porcelain for years. He arrived at about 9 a.m., sold every piece as he opened it up, and by 9.30 was left with a lot of money in his pocket and nothing left to do but to go home. He had sold at many times the prices he had paid, but he was still too cheap.

The same excitement still exists at the Wednesday and Saturday markets. On Wednesday, the dealers are there at the break of day, but Saturday starts at a more civilised time – around 9 am.

3

The time had come, in early 1960, to think about an official opening day and what we could do to promote interest. My art shop manager suggested an open-air art show, and that was adopted as a good idea by the CPTA. For an art show we would need some display stands and, of course, a lot of pictures. We placed an advertisement in an art magazine and also sought the help of the Islington Art Society. As a result, we were swamped with pictures, some of them extremely good and others extremely bad. The Islington Art Society, under the wing of George Bunting who was also hiring a stall, were very cooperative. They joined the selection committee and came up with some good suggestions, based on their own experience.

The stands proved to be a difficult obstacle. In order to show all the submitted works, we would need a lot of display space. We designed a stand in the form of an 'A' frame to which we attached two eight-foot by four-foot, hardboard sheets, one each side. We estimated that we would require eight of these. Then came the question of 'What if it rains?' This was solved by fitting four 'horns' to each stand and stretching transparent plastic sheeting across. The finished stands were very heavy and bulky, and we would have been in a dreadful fix knowing where to garage them, without the help of Alec Catt, who owns Beck's at Nos 22-26 Camden Passage (one of the few remaining original CPTA members still in business in Camden Passage). He had a small lean-to shed which had recently become vacant. It had for years been occupied by the 'cats-meat' man, a diminutive Italian who spent his whole life cutting up and delivering meat, wrapped in newspaper, for the local pets. I know that our own cat knew exactly when he was due to deliver his meat, and was on duty at the door at the appointed time. The shed was only about six feet wide, but it was quite deep and we managed to house all the stands in it.

Things were coming together, and the next consideration was publicity. The *Islington Gazette* and the *Hackney Gazette*, our local papers, were well aware of what was going on, and had been very supportive and promised us full coverage. In fact, they ran stories immediately, speaking of the enterprise of the shopkeepers of Camden Passage. The *Islington Gazette* even referred to it as 'Payton Place', but only because of the similarity to the name of the American TV show – there were no such 'goings-on' in Camden Passage as far as I know. This created lots more interest locally, but we needed to be known nationally.

A date had to be fixed for the official opening, and after much deliberation, including finding out the best non-rainy month, September 3rd was chosen.

A letter was addressed to the then Mayor of Islington, Alderman Agnes Seeley, asking if she would carry out the official opening, and she graciously and enthusiastically accepted.

At a meeting of the CPTA, I asked if anyone knew a 'name' who would take part in the opening. Arnold Cawthrow, Big Chief I-Spy, knew that fine comedy actor and producer, Michael Medwin, and Arnold promised to ask him to be part of the ceremony (he subsequently generously agreed). Someone suggested that a beautiful blonde could be an attraction. They had seen such a creature being weighed in pennies for a charity. It so happened that the owner of the Angel Bedding shop in the Arcade, which used to be where the Angel bus-stop now is, was married to Sheree Winton, a well-made 'dumb blonde' with theatrical connections. This man was quite a bit older than his beautiful wife, and he could not believe his luck in owning her. However, his life was made miserable at the thought of ever losing his treasure. I asked him if he would ask her if she would consent to being weighed for charity – all in aid of the Spastics Society – and she happily agreed.

So, the stage was set for the opening except for one

important factor – we needed publicity – and not one of us knew how to approach and interest the National Press. I was much concerned about this and pestered eveyone I knew, without any success. Time was rushing by and the opening day getting uncomfortably close, and here we were at the beginning of August and still no clues about publicity – we certainly could not afford a public relations firm to do it for us.

Then Joy Bradbury, one of my stallholders (a rosy-faced lady who specialized in perfect elocution), told me that she had read that Daphne Guinness had just moved to Islington and was, she thought, in a house opposite the Regent Canal, just at the back of Camden Passage. Daphne Guinness was on the reporting staff of the William Hickey column of the *Daily Express* – the sort of column that is virtually full of stories containing *names*. The poor man's society column *à la Tatler*. I soon found the address in Vincent Terrace, and one evening, my heart in my mouth, knocked on the door of No.6 Vincent Terrace. The beautiful Daphne opened the door, and I quickly told her what was happening in Camden Passage and how I was desperate to know how to get some National Press publicity, and asked could she help, please?

'You don't want me, you want my husband Perry,' she said. 'Come in.'

Perry welcomed me warmly, and they both listened to my story with intense interest. Perry said he would be glad to help and asked me a lot of questions. I departed from them late that night feeling much elated, not only because I thought Camden Passage was to get the help I had asked for, but because I felt I had made new friends.

Perry was employed by the British Broadcasting Corporation, where he was responsible for the publicity. A tall, dark, good-looking quietly-spoken man, Perry is of the famous Guinness brewing family, but not the branch with wealth. He had served below-deck in the navy, and was intensely interested in people and events. I suspect he had not much time or interest in 'Society'.

The next couple of weeks were to serve to show me what could be done when there was a story to 'sell' to the Press. We had conferences evey night until we came to the weekend before the opening day, which was to be a Saturday. Perry unfolded to me his plan of action.

A press release was to be hand-delivered (by us) to the Press at different times for each newspaper, starting on the Friday night and extending over the weekend. This release was designed to appeal to the snob – 'everyone is a snob of some sort' said Perry. The latter asked who, on the occasion of the opening of Camden Passage Antique Centre and the Art Show, was the most important person in Islington? Was it Basil Spence (later to be knighted for his design of Coventry Cathedral), or Professor Parkinson (*Times* crossword), or Raymond Mortimer (famous art critic), or even Flora Robson, the famous actress? All of these people lived in a small oasis in Islington, called Canonbury. (A visit to Canonbury is a *must* for a visitor, with fine Georgian houses around Canonbury Square; Canonbury House, where the late Sir Basil Spence lived, and Canonbury Tower, full of history. The rest of Islington was at that time out of fashion, with most of the houses in the lovely squares severely run-down and occupied as tenements by a number of families. These people could be contacted on their various floors by the number of knocks on the knocker – 'Number 19, four knocks').

Well, to return to the press release, here we were barely mentioning Camden Passage, the antiques or the Art Show, but instead doing a spot of shameful name-dropping! I had enough sense to keep my thoughts to myself, on the principle that we were getting expert advice, generously given, by someone who obviously knew what he was doing. Public relations experts move in a mysterious way, their wonders to perform.

The press releases were handed in at all the National dailies and then, at another given time, to all the evening papers, and at yet another time to the Sunday papers, some of the deliveries taking place at two o'clock in the morning. We were finally finished on Sunday evening, one week before the opening.

'Now go home, and DO NOT LEAVE YOUR PHONE,' ordered Perry.

We had not long to wait. Monday morning, the *News Chronicle* (since defunct) printed a pretty garbled account of what was contained in the press release. Then the telephone started to ring in earnest, and just about every media outlet wanted to know what was going on. I had been tutored by Perry that a group of people getting together to do something was news, while the 'I did it' response was NOT news. I therefore told the reporters how all the small shopkeepers had turned out, night after night, to paint each others' shops, concrete the bombed sites and generally cooperate. They liked what they heard, and very soon the Passage was buzzing with reporters, photographers and TV cameras. A few times I heard one of the shopkeepers being interviewed. 'Whose idea was it?' they were asked. The answer made it pretty clear that, if the whole idea was not theirs, most of it was! I said nothing, but stuck to my story of the community effort.

Every day, something appeared in the National Press, and there were a number of radio interviews. 'The *Star*' evening paper ran an article headed, 'They're the new Angels of Islington.' This somehow invented the 'Islington Set' – Sir Basil Spence, Sir Philip Hendy (National Gallery Director), Dame Flora Robson, playwright Arnold Wesker, Michael, the dress designer, and Arthur Peterson, Chairman of the Prison Commissioners – who, they said, were determined to preserve Camden Passage. These names came from Perry Guinness's press release, and it is very doubtful if any of these illustrious people had any interest in preserving Camden Passage at that time or, indeed, knew of its existence. This certainly came later.

The Times, on September 1st, just two days before the official opening, ran an article below a picture of Camden Passage. This article gave a true view of what had been going on, what was going to happen and what the future possible held. Full credit was given to the traders of Camden Passage for their enterprise, and the paint firm was given credit for producing the painting plan! The *News Chronicle* printed a column which dealt in the main with Perry Guinness, his kinship with the Earl of Iveagh, and his previous connection with Chelsea Cloisters. They then listed the 'Canonbury' celebrities, names in heavy type, saying that Perry was convinced that there was an Islington Set – but they failed to mention Camden Passage at all!

The BBC ran a number of news items, as did ITN news. Television coverage was given by ATV Channel 9 on September 2nd.

A party had been arranged to take place immediately after the opening ceremony at 11 a.m., and Perry Guinness had invited quite a lot of celebrities, most of whom had accepted. There were also many guests of the CPTA, so it looked like being a big 'do'. There was only one place to hold such a large gathering, and that was in my home at 106 High Street (which is now occupied by that fine and famous restaurant, 'Fredericks'). I had moved into these premises in late 1957. Before then, it was a public house – it had been called The Duke of Sussex since 1820, and was previously called The Gun as far back as 1700. The brewers closed down many of the pubs that had become uneconomical and this one, a Watneys pub, had gone downhill with the rest of Camden Passage in the 1950s. On the first floor, there was a very large room which had been the club room, and it was there that the party was to be held.

It became obvious that 11a.m. Saturday 3rd September, 1960, was going to be a BIG day, not, perhaps as big as 11 a.m. 3rd September, 1939, when England declared war on Germany, but, judging by the interest shown and the many enthusiastic articles that had already appeared in the National Press, pretty important just the same. Every shopkeeper had been asked to be ready to get up early that day and help with the art stands. Each shop was allotted a number of paintings to store overnight and asked to be ready to bring them out first thing. D-day was approaching. . . .

There had been about twelve months of planning and hard work put into the transformation of Camden Passage, all of it directed to this all-important day – September 3rd, 1960. To judge by the great amount of interest generated by the media in the National Press, radio and television, we could expect a very large crowd. It was thought wise to alert the local police to this possibility, especially as the Mayor of Islington was to officiate.

A few hundred posters heralding the great event had been distributed far and wide. While they were being printed by Peacock & Son, the printers at 18/20 Camden

Passage whose business is still there, we had a call from the Town Hall telling us that an objection had been raised about the use of the pavement area for an art show. 'Who has complained?' I asked. 'Mr. Peacock' was the reply! I had thought that there was some sort of ethical conduct with printers as with doctors and lawyers, so that information provided for printing was confidential. As it turned out, the Council would not support the complaint and we took it all in good part as old Peacock, then about seventy-nine years old, was quite a character. A tall, large-boned man with an ugly face with large nose and big, wide mouth, he had appeared on the clubs and music halls as a stand-up comic in the past, and was always good for a factual story about Camden Passage when he was a boy, for he was born and bred in close proximity to it. He ruled his small printing company, consisting of his two sons and himself, with a rod of iron. He would have nothing to do with trying to improve Camden Passage, but his older son, Ron, quietly promised me that when he was eventually in charge, he would convert the shopfronts into shops. He was as good as his word once his father had died, and he has converted the whole of the ground floor to an indoor market while the printing shop still carries on in the basement.

We had threaded coloured lights all along Camden Passage, zig-zagging from one side to another, and the effect was very cosy. (The Council did not like them and told us to take them down but we ignored them. They were the responsibility of Stan Owen, who was Beck's manager and an electrician, so there was no danger).

A rostrum was erected outside the then-empty shop at 12 Camden Passage, on the corner of Charlton Place. Alec Catt's amplification wizard, again Stan Owen, promised to provide a microphone and amplifier for the ceremony.

The room at 106 High Street was to accommodate the reception which was to follow the opening ceremony, and this was prepared for the event the night before. Peter Sheel, a society artist whose works had included portraits of King Hussein of Jordan, the Duchess of Windsor, Talullah Bankhead, Vivien Leigh, Arlene Dahl and Kay Kendall had been invited by Perry to display portraits of some of his subjects in the reception room. The wine and orange juice was in place, and a large number of glasses had been hired. Volunteer bartenders were due to arrive at the appointed time.

A number of local celebrities had decided to run a special antiques stall in aid of charity – the Spastics Society – notable Larry Gordon (the choreographer of the Television Toppers), Valerie Brooks, Phillip King and Johnny Baron. A painting by actor Michael Denison was to be auctioned, Russ Conway had presented signed record albums and photographs.

Two distinguished artists put on an exhibition of their work in the Art Shop at 110 High Street. The two were partners and worked as potters, in oils, water colours, wood-carvings, ceramics and sculpture, and I am sure you will appreciate the name of one of them – Francois Xavier Gonzales Angello-de-Cauchserra (a marvellous warm-hearted bearded eccentric) Beryl Hardman (Beryl died in the late 60s but not before instructing Angello to go find another girl-friend).

Eveything was in apple-pie order ready for the opening day.

The Times on 1st September wrote: 'How much more worthwhile it is to preserve such places (Camden Passage) when their own inhabitants, like the united traders of Camden Passage, take so fine a part in adapting what is old and beautiful to the modern way of life.'

4

On the great day, I awoke at 5.30 a.m. to find that it was pouring with rain. Not the normal rain experienced in London, but a tropical downpour of incessant rain – 'cats and dogs'. This was a disaster of enormous magnitude for the Passage. It looked very much as if the work of the past twelve months, which had included painting, concreting, planning, pleading (with the council), persuading, cajolling, picture selecting, stall letting, sleepless night-ing, was wasted. But there was nothing for it but to soldier on, put on raincoats and get those A-frame art stands out of the shed and set them up along the centre of the Passage. We were all completely drenched within a few minutes, but once you are so wet that you cannot get any wetter, it matters not. We then fixed the horns onto the frames and stretched the sheets of plastic across. Everyone came from his shop and set up the oil paintings and watercolours onto the stands, umbrellas in evidence everywhere. In no time at all, the plastic sheets were being filled with gallons and gallons of rainwater and bellying alarmingly, threatening to burst or collapse all over the paintings. Broomsticks provided the solution to this problem, and a small squad of volunteers, consisting of shopkeepers and a few of the artists involved, walked up and down the stands, pushing upwards in the middle, causing a huge torrent of water to splash onto the pavement. That was the pattern for the next few hours, with the vigilantes running up and down dislodging the bellying plastic covers.

By 10.30 the rain was still coming down relentlessly, and I had to leave the water patrol while I went to change into something respectable as befits meeting the Mayor,

Michael Medwin and Sheree Winton. As I was leaving the scene of the disaster, a police inspector arrived with a number of uniformed policemen. He saw the terrible state of affairs, and said that he would do his best to help by putting all of his Bobbies at the top of Charlton Place in Upper Street.

'A crowd of our chaps always brings the curious,' he said. Nice of him, but there were not too many curious enough to brave that rain, although it certainly did have an effect a little later in the day.

At five minutes to eleven, I stood under an umbrella in Upper Street at the appointed spot to greet the Mayor. The rain eased a little. At one minute to eleven the rain stopped! At eleven the Mayor, Alderman Agnes Seeley, arrived, and I escorted her to my house, to find that Michael Medwin had arrived with Sheree Winton.

'Well,' I said to them, 'someone up there is relenting at last. I shall be surprised if there are many people who've turned up, but all we can do is go and find out.' We set off to walk towards the rostrum in as dignified a manner as possible, the Mayor accompanied by her mace-bearer, and Michael Medwin, missing the puddles as much as possible.

There were some one hundred people waiting – ninety-nine more that I thought there might be under the circumstances, for the events of the morning had done nothing to give me any optimism, having become convinced the powers of evil were rampant. We mounted the rostrum and I prepared to make the first public speech I had ever made in my life. The microphone stood before me; my notes were in my hand.

'Ladies and . . .' I started and abruptly stopped. No sound at all from the microphone! Stan Owen was meddling with the amplifier. He shook his head to signify that it was as drowned as everything else. 'I shall have to shout like a barrow-boy,' I said to myself.

'WELCOME TO CAMDEN PASSAGE-ON-SEA,' I yelled, coming eye to eye with the magnificent and eloquent broadcaster, television personality and Member of Parliament, Tom Driberg! After what I had been through that morning, I threw caution to the winds, lost my nervousness and delivered my opening speech of welcome from a damp

The official opening of Camden Passage on September 3rd 1960. Agnes Seeley, Mayor of Islington and Michael Medwin are greeted by John Payton.

piece of paper to an ever-increasing crowd. People were appearing from everywhere! I thanked the Mayor for attending this important moment in the history of Camden Passage and, indeed, of Islington. I thanked Sheree Winton for honouring us with her beautiful presence (I came eye to eye with her husband at that moment, and tried to reassure him by a look that his prize possession was safe with me), and I thanked Michael Medwin. I then introduced the Worshipful Mayor of Islington to perform the official opening.

Agnes Seely proved to be a charming lady. She had done her homework, and knew exactly what had been going on in Camden Passage. We had become accustomed in Islington to not expect too much of our elected Councillors. Islington is now and was then a strong Labour borough, and it used to come as no surprise when a Mayor made a speech of a rather low standard, probably in a very uneducated voice. But here was a lady who obviously was used to calling a spade a spade, and could do so with fine eloquence.

The Mayor applauded the enterprise of the Camden Passage Traders' Association. She had always associated the word 'quality' with Camden Passage, and liked to think of it as Quality Street. She was sure that there was a great

Guests at the inaugural cocktail party . . . Daphne Guinness, fashion journalist, Sheree Winton, film and Television celebrity, Leigh Underhill, Camden Passage Antique Dealer and Diana Fisher, daughter-in-law of The Archbishop of Canterbury.

future for the area, and told her audience that she would always be supportive.

Once the applause had died down, a bouquet was presented to the Mayor by little Valerie Friend. Then Michael Medwin thanked the Mayor for honouring Camden Passage with her presence, and followed with a witty and hilariously funny speech which set the mood for the next event, which was to weigh the lovely Sherree on some large scales we had borrowed. I asked for pennies to match her weight, and John Friend started off the collection with a five-shilling bag of them (sixty pieces, for those unfamiliar with the old currency).

Having got the proceedings moving along, I took the Mayor away to open the reception – nobody was allowed in until she arrived. We got back to 106 High Street to find a long queue formed outside. Every guest was asked to sign a visitors book, and this record of the opening party is now in the Camden Passage archives.

While in The Passage Michael Medwin was keeping the crowd amused with his easy wit, and Sherree Winton was keeping the crowd bemused with her lovely looks, and the pennies were rolling in to try and match her weight, the party was proving to be a great success. Camden Passage was well and truly launched, and the party was such that there was precious little liquid refreshment left by the time the last stragglers departed.

There was one duty left to the Mayor, and that was to make a formal inspection of the art works, many of which had already been decorated with a small red sticker which indicated that they were sold. By this time the Passage was milling with people, and the various fund-raising activities for charity were reporting success.

One of those artists who was to later achieve great success was Sheila Flynn, to whom I shall return later.

The ensuing publicity played a large part in the establishment of Camden Passage as a major antique centre. The Press was never without an article or a mention of Camden Passage, and it became very noticeable that the Chelsea crowd was taking a lot of interest in Islington. A press release by Perry in early December accelerated the process of change. He asked, in his release, 'who is the most notable person in Islington?' and trotted out our favourites – Sir Basil Spence, Raymond Mortimer, Sir Philip Hendy, Flora Robson, Beatrice Lehmann etc. The rather astonishing result from this was that the Press started to run stories on the theme that Islington was the new Chelsea. As a result, just before Christmas of 1960, the locals were asked to part with their houses at prices which they had never dreamed possible. These houses were then gutted and rebuilt internally, retaining their Georgian or Victorian facades.

Prices of Islington freeholds began to rocket (but were still comparatively cheap compared with Kensington or Chelsea) as Islington became recognized as having such great potential – very close to the City, yet set on a hill where the air was hopefully fresher. Houses which were once fine needed only restoring to their previous elegance.

Camden Passage, in this short three months following the opening, was now filled with antique shops.

Aspects of Camden Passage. Left: Mr John Payton studies
the plan for the Pierrepont Arcade of permanent shops to
be built on the cleared site.
Right: Stallholders are prepared to sit through the long
cold day.

It was essential to maintain a good flow of publicity in the
National Press and on the television for, otherwise, how was
the world to know about Camden Passage? Perry Guinness
worked tirelessly and also tutored me in the art, so that I
was able to send out press releases at intervals. I became so
enthusiastic that I think I reported too regularly. One day, I
followed up one of the press releases with a telephone call,

A cycle shop faces the new shops and market stalls
across the passage.

and was connected to a sub-editor. Did he receive my release, I asked him? Yes and all the others, too – so many that he tended to ignore them, he replied. I got the message, and only sent them out when there was something important enough to warrant attention.

It was in March 1961 that Perry Guinness pulled off a great publicity coup for Camden Passage.

The fine art centre of London is in Old Bond Street, where all the famous dealers and auctioneers have their shops and rooms. Qantas, the Australian airline (Queensland and Northern Territories Air Service, in case you did not know) has its London headquarters on the corner of Old Bond Street and Piccadilly. Here, homesick Australians and interested customers can browse through Australian newspapers and publications in the Reading Room at the ground floor level. There is a basement which consists of a large open-plan area, and this was used for art exhibitions, its luxurious appointments including free-standing double-sided screens and felt-lined wall panels ideal for the display of paintings. It is probable that under the terms of their lease, Qantas were required to maintain these areas as an art gallery. The London public relations manager, Julia Bradbery, was responsible for arranging occasional art shows in the basement, her bosses obviously believing that this would attract the attention of art dealers passing on the way to the Old Bond Street brigade.

'What,' you may ask, 'has this to do with Camden Passage?' Patience . . .

'Blue Peter', produced by Verity Lambert, was a highly successful childrens' programme which appeared on BBC Television (if you do not remember 'Blue Peter', you will know Verity Lambert's work as Executive Producer of Arthur Daley and Terry's series 'Minder'). The audience of 'Blue Peter' had been invited to submit pictures depicting what they thought would represent typical scenes in Australia. A similar audience in Australia, watchers of 'The Argonauts', an equally successful long-running childrens' TV programme, was asked to paint what they thought to be their idea of the United Kingdom. The best pictures submitted by the UK and Australian audiences were combined into an exhibition which, after being on show at

Qantas headquarters in Piccadilly, were to be transported and exhibited from one capital city to another throughout the world. Perry was asked to look after all the other arrangements.

The exhibition at Qantas headquarters was more successful than anything previously organized on the premises. It was well publicized on the 'Blue Peter' programme and would have been attended by the family and friends of every UK exhibitor, but it offered little more than can be seen at an open day of any primary school. Julia Bradbery, the Qantas manager, was ecstatic, and it was at this point that Perry asked her if she would like him to follow on with another art exhibition which would present the best of the work by London's street artists, whose work had hitherto been seen only in London streets, these streets having since become tourist attractions, but never in a gallery or an indoor exhibition. The occupations of the artists would vary from managing director of a cigarette company to a Lyons waitress, a night watchman, a Smithfield market meat porter and an ex-convict. An opportunity to show their works in comfortable surroundings in the very heart of London's fine art centre would attract a large number of visitors and considerable publicity.

Julia was a bit nervous about the idea, but said she would submit the proposal to her bosses. In the event, she was astonished when they agreed.

When Perry came to me with the idea I, too, was not a little nonplussed until he pointed out that this was an opportunity to promote Camden Passage from the heart of the most fashionable and central quarter of London. When he also explained that the exhibition title would include the words 'Camden Passage' and would present yet another opportunity to attract media attention, I became most enthusiastic.

This was not the whole story of Perry's master plan. He wanted an opening that would be the equal of any other happening in Old Bond Street – sophisticated drinks, cocktail food and an official catalogue giving full details of each artist, names, addresses, telephone numbers and biographical details (so that the Press could follow up if they wished, and also to enable buyers or potential buyers to maintain contact with exhibitors after the show), but nothing that would associate the exhibition or the exhibitors with church halls or a charity do. He also wanted the opening to be conducted by a genuine celebrity, who would be invited to select a work of art from the exhibition in lieu of a fee. Our artists' self-esteem would be lifted, and the occasion would have added interest.

At this stage Perry passed the organization of the artists and art work to me. My first problem was to find out how we were going to pay for the champagne, cocktail food and catalogue! There was no money in the Camden Passage kitty in 1961, and my members would have had forty fits if I had suggested going round with the proverbial hat.

I called in George Bunting, the chairman of the Islington Art Circle and a most helpful person. We devised a simple plan which he was sure would succeed. We would make a small charge per square foot of space to every artist who was accepted for inclusion in the exhibition, and this would cover the cost of the reception and catalogue. But that was not quite enough, as we had to cover the cost of the painting that would be selected by our celebrity guest. We added to our rules that the selected painting would be charged at a special low price, and this cost would be split between the rest of the exhibiting artists, again according to the space they occupied.

Once the word was circulated among the artists' community, there was no shortage of willing participants. We formed a selection committee and were very severe about discarding any work which was considered unsuitable – this is a very difficult and unrewarding task, which can foster a few enemies in the form of rejected artists.

Perry, meanwhile, had asked Peter Dimmock and Polly Elwes, whose recent courtship and wedding had attracted big publicity, to perform the opening ceremony, and they had agreed. Peter was head of BBC Television's Outside Broadcasts Department and well-known to the public as host of the very popular prime-time 'Sports Report'. Polly, from an aristocratic Roman Catholic backgound which included many distinguished persons, one of whom was a Royal portrait painter, Simon Elwes, was one of the first female reporters employed on television news and current

Miss Polly Elwes, who opened the Camden Passage Art Exhibition at the QANTAS Gallery on Monday, with her husband Peter Dimmock, looking at the painting they chose. The Camden Passage Association presented the picture to her. (See page 62)

affairs programme – a beautiful and much admired lady.

The date was fixed as March 20th to April 1st. Invitations for the special private opening and viewing at 6.30 on the 20th, went out to many celebrities and to the media on an RSVP basis, and it quickly became clear that we were going to have to provide a lot of refreshment!

There was a large and distinguished crowd of people that I looked down at from the position half-way up the stairs leading from the basement to the ground floor, where I introduced the Camden Passage Exhibition, thanked Qanta and introduced and thanked Polly Elwes and Peter Dimmock. I recall being introduced to Lord Reith, head of the

BBC, and to many other well-known people, but I must confess that the rest was a blur of excited artists surrounded by reporters and TV cameras. In a very short time, the little red stickers which denote a sale had appeared on a number of paintings.

The picture chosen by Peter and Polly as their reward received considerable media attention. It was one of several oil paintings and lino cuts of animals and birds by Sheila Flinn, an artist who lived close to Camden Passage. Her style was distinctive, and the colours which she employed were most attractive. Strangely enough, as luck would have it, her work looked absolutely outstanding in black and white when shown on television or in newspaper photographs, and was widely used by the media to illustrate stories about the exhibition, giving an impression of quality to an occasion which might otherwise have been dismissed as an amusing idea but not worthy of serious attention.

By the end of the exhibition, to the best of my recollection, there were only two works which remained unsold – one gaudy abstract item which should never have been accepted in the first place, and a sculpture made of bits of wire and coloured balls which failed to excite the same interest in prospective purchasers as existed in the artist's bosom. In addition, some of the artists whose works were fully sold received commissions to produce further works. The star artist was certainly Sheila Flinn.

Sheila sold every one of her small paintings on the first day, and the two remaining large paintings were purchased soon after by Cary Grant and Zsa Zsa Gabor, both of whom were staying in London independently at the time and were inspired to visit the exhibition by the media coverage. The work bought by Zsa Zsa was unfortunately lost a year later, when a fire destroyed her Beverley Hills home.

A visitor representing a richly endowed religious university in the United States was so impressed by Sheila's work that he commissioned her to paint a picture which included every bird and animal mentioned in the Bible as a major illustration for a new edition and also to hang in a prominent public position.

But the cake was certainly taken by a London buyer who acted for a Toronto, Canada, department store which specialized in providing an interior design and decoration service. It is reported that this store was so popular and successful that most Toronto homes of executives had a similar appearance, as it enabled all the Jones's to keep up with one another without the need for any personal effort. The London buyer was greatly impressed by Sheila Flinn's work and gave her a commission to supply the store with *all* works that she produced, this order remaining for as long as she could continue to paint! I cannot report on whether the store or Sheila expired first.

A friend was kind enough to buy one of Sheila Flinn's works as a belated wedding present for Perry Guinness, and he bought a few under his own steam as well as some of the works of other artists, all of which proudly hang in his Sydney home as a reminder of one of his great public relations triumphs which were to have such an impact on the future of Camden Passage.

5

We pressed our A-frames into service again when, only two weeks after the close of our Qantas success, on April 15 – 23rd, 1961, Camden Passage held its Second Art Exhibition.

On this occasion the fine actor, Arthur Howard – brother of the late Leslie Howard – kindly undertook the official opening, and this was followed by a function at 106 High Street. Arthur Howard is a delightful person. One of his endearing roles was with comedian Jimmy Edwards as Mr Pettigrew, the timid schoolmaster in the television series 'Whack-o'. Our stalwart supporter, Mayor Agnes Seeley, attended in her official capacity. Mayor Seeley, hearing that one of the artists exhibiting was a direct descent of John Milton, said 'Milton wrote *Paradise Lost* and *Paradise Regained*. This applies to Camden Passage, as it has certainly been regained.'

In order to bring in some crowds, we hired tall, American-accented bagpiper George Alexander to firstly pipe Arthur Howard and the Mayor of Islington to the rostrum, and then to march himself over to Chapel Market and along Upper Street. So that the public would know what it was in aid of, we also hired a sandwich-board man from an agency. They sent along a small down-and-out man with his board on to which we pinned our prepared notices.

'You follow the piper' I told him. 'Keep about ten yards behind, and go wherever he goes.'

Off went George, a fine figure of a man in his full Scottish regalia, followed by the small, scruffy man. From time to time, the swirl of the pipes came floating across from the distance, but I did not see them again for a couple of hours,

Left to right: Highland Piper and Publicity Manager for
Camden Passage Trades Association.

Professor Bronowski points out the finer points of art to
Daphne Guinness.

when George arrived back. As soon as he had deflated his
pipes, he said with a twinkle in his eye: 'I don't think our
sandwich man likes the pipes. You told him to stay ten
yards behind, but he got further and further back. Every
time I marked time for him to catch up, he stayed where he
was, and no amount of waving would bring him any closer!'
In fact, our little man came along a few minutes later – a
good 200 yards behind George!

Scotsmen are supposedly on the mean side, but I was
greatly touched when I paid George and he handed the
money straight back for donation to the Spastics Society, to
whom we donated the profits of the day.

Our guests, among others, were the diminutive, brilliant
scientist and television personality, Professor Bronowski,
his wife and two young daughters, and Peter Dimmock and

Comedian Stanley Baxter opens the 3rd Art Exhibition
in 1961.

Polly Elwes. With the weather being kind to us, a very large crowd turned out.

While we were doing our tour of inspection of the paintings, Prof. Bronowski gave his opinion on them ; there were some paintings there which he abhorred, saying they were dreadful 'pot-boilers'.

'These are not art' he said. 'They are just painted for making money.' But on the whole, the standard was high and some paintings were outstanding, many of the artists who had shown in Piccadilly having frenziedly replenished their stocks.

Back at 106, the Bronowski children were told that they could go and choose any painting they liked. Perry Guinness asked the Professor whether that was not a trifle dangerous.

'No,' said Bronowski in his most scientific manner, 'it is the way you bring up your children that has the influence on their judgement throughout their life.' He said a lot more on that subject, as he was wont to do in his television series.

Some time later, back came the children with their chosen artworks – the very pot boilers that the Professor deplored so much!

☆   ☆   ☆

Our Third Open-Air Art Exhibition took place from 16–23 September, 1961, and at the same time we exhibited entries for a Junior Art Competition for children aged seven to fifteen, with prizes in three groups.

The hilariously funny actor/comedian, Glaswegian Stanley Baxter, an Islington resident himself, kindly opened this exhibition and had his audience in fits. This was again a very successful event and brought a lot of publicity and therefore new faces to the Passage.

The Islington childrens' art contest proved to be a very popular event, and many hundreds of paintings were submitted.

We had asked the eminent art critic, Eric Newton, if he would judge the children's competition. He not only agreed but asked two others to help him – writer and art critic, literary editor of *Nation* and *Sunday Times* and member of the

Left to right: Mrs J. Payton, Arthur Howard, Mrs Bronowski, John Payton, Agnes Seeley, Mayor of Islington, and Derek de Marney star of 'Dangerous Moonlight.'

Royal Fine Art Commission Raymond Mortimer, and a well-known collector and art connoisseur, Edward le Bas. It was arranged that they would assemble for the judging at Eric Newton's house, which was in one of the Victorian squares behind Sadler's Wells Theatre.

All entries were piled into the back of my station-wagon, and I picked up Raymond Mortimer from his lovely Georgian home in Canonbury Place. This very charming gentleman spent a lot of his time at his cottage in a Dorset village. He said he dreaded opening his front door whenever he returned from being away in Dorset, because he had a small Renoir painting in his hall and he wondered if it would still be there, there being so many robberies taking place. I think he was contemplating disposing of it just to be rid of the worry.

We arrived at Eric Newton's house, and I unloaded the pile of paintings into the large lounge room, noting as I went in that an enormous Bratby painting dominated the hall – Bratby squeezed his paint straight out of the tube onto the canvas, and I remember envying the lucky art shop who supplied him his paints and wishing it were my own that had the contract.

There followed in the next few hours a totally absorbing selection committee operation which would have qualified for the judging of the annual British Accademy. There was not a single entry that was not perused – I was holding them up two at a time – and I was impressed to note that there was a unanimity of opinion among the three eminent people.

'No.- No.- No.- Put that one on the side, don't you agree? No.- No.- I say, that has something – put it with the other one.'

Finally, there were about twenty-five paintings selected, and they went very carefully through them, discussing each one. There was a final and unanimous decision in favour of one picture by a lad of twelve years old. Then a second and a third winner selected.

I would like to pay tribute to these gentlemen, all of whom were foremost in the field of art and could have had very little spare time, yet there was no thought among them other than to do a thorough and honest job over what was, after all, a very minor competition. The quality displayed by them which was so impressive to me was that of humility. Perhaps only truly great men can afford humility.

For the prize-giving, we asked another of Islington's noted residents, Geoffrey Adams, to officiate. Geoffrey Adams is a fine actor, and at that time was well-known for his portrayal of PC Lauderdale in the series 'Dixon of Dock Green'. Geoffrey brought with him his lovely wife, who played the part of a woman PC in the same series.

Our next Art Exhibition took place in 1962, from May 26th – June 2nd. Again, we ran an Islington Children's Art Contest and displayed the entries alongside adult artists' works. Despite bad weather the exhibition was a roaring success. So was the ensuing (inevitable) party, but this time it was held at the newly opened John's Restaurant at No. 2 Camden Passage (whose arrival in Camden Passage will be

The Mayor (Stan) and Mayoress of Islington presenting prizes to the winners of the Islington Children's Art Contest.

dealt with in a later chapter). Our stalwart supporters, Peter Dimmock and Polly Elwes, were present, and this time they were accompanied by John Spencer Churchill, who looks so much like Winston, Derek de Marney, star of 'Dangerous Moonlight', and that generous music expert, Philip Bate, who donated his rare collection of antique musical wind instruments to Oxford University. That Phil Bate is not a rich man makes his gift the more admirable, for they are worth a very considerable amount of money. Those great theatrical photographers, Agnus McBean and Hams Wild, both Islingtonians, were there too.

The children's art competition prize-giving was arranged to take place on a weekday from a rostrum erected for the occasion outside Peacock the printer's premises. The presentation was to be made by the Worshipful Mayor of Islington.

A large crowd of children and parents gathered in Camden Passage. I escorted the Mayor and Mayoress, his wife, to the rostrum and introduced them.

The speech that followed hardly fitted into any scenario

remotely connected with the arts. Our Mayor was not what you might call an educated man, and was incapable of doing justice to the situation. However, this did not stop him – he had obviously learned in politics that once you have the floor, you had better hold it for as long as possible, or someone else might say something. That you have nothing to say does not appear to enter into it. He went on and on and on.

'Now listen ere, you kids. These good people ave set up this competition and gone to a lot of trouble, and you oughta be grateful.' He went on in that vein, and on and on and on . . . there was much shuffling of feet among the captive audience; I thought he would never end. Then, halfway through a sentence, her Worshipful Mayoress, seated at his side, spoke:

'That's enough, Stan.' Stan sat down immediately, mid-sentence. After the presentations, I took them to 106 for drinks. They were genuine people but, unlike our Agnes Seeley of a few years before, they were not up to an art occasion.

But only a few weeks later we were to meet again.

A certain worthy charity organizer hit on the brainwave of inviting the high society of Islington (anyone who might have some money, inlcuded with the Sir Basil Spences and Raymond Mortimers) to a Wine & Cheese event, to take place at the Islington Central Library in Holloway Road. This library has a good sized hall, suitable for concerts. Some 250 worthy people of Islington turned up by invitation and were ushered into the hall which had all the chairs bunched in the centre, leaving a very wide aisle all round. This was to prove unfortunate.

Up got one speaker to the rostrum, which was also set up with a wide gap between it and the audience. He went on for some time about the charity and then introduced another speaker, who went on about the same sort of subject. The wide gangway all round the chairs made furtive escape impossible – if ever there was a captive audience, this was it. This speaker then introduced yet another speaker who, when he had finished, introduced our Stan, the Mayor. If Camden Passage's art event was a little beyond Stan, this gathering was miles away. However, nothing daunted, he started on in a similar vein to the Camden Passage speech. And he went on, and on, and on. This time, his lady wife was too far away to issue the 'That's enough' order, but he eventually ran out of steam.

The audience had to stay where it was until the Mayor and Mayoress made their dignified exit in order that they could be at the head of the reception line for the wine and cheese part of the event, something everyone was now looking forward to with fervent interest. Many, myself included, had thoughts of being amongst the wine and cheese a lot earlier than this.

It came to my turn to be presented.

'Oh!' says the Mayoress, 'It's Mr Payton. You remember, Stan, we took wain with im a couple of weeks ago.' I don't think he did – remember, I mean.

6

One day in 1962, I was on my rounds, collecting the two-and-sixpences (now being spent on advertising), and I approached Harry Levey who ran the gramophone record and sewing machine shop (he kept only the old treadle Singer models in which he specialized and became, I think, the only place in London that could service them). The shops – he had two – were at 33 and 35 Camden Passage. He was then about seventy years old and lived with his brother and sister on the premises, carrying on a business previously run by his father as far back as 1860. His brother used to set off up the road with a light rucksack on his back. I stopped to talk to him once as he was walking towards the Angel underground station. He told me he was just on his way to Brazil this time! 'This time?' I queried, thoroughly bewildered.

'Yes,' he said, 'I go somewhere every year. Sometimes I am away for six months. I've been all over the world.' 'Is that all you take with you?' I asked. 'Yes,' he answered, 'I've got a change of shirt, socks and underpants and my toilet kit, and that's all you need. Cheerio, see you in a few months time.' And off he went to Brazil, via the Angel underground.

Harry Levey was a tall, well-padded man. He had a large, round face and sported a pathetically inadequate flat ginger wig which sat conspicuously upon his bald head. He kept himself very much to himself, and appeared not to like anyone in uniform. Old Mr Peacock, whose printing works was right opposite, told me that when a couple of ambulance men came to take his (Peacock's) wife for some therapy and they had to wait as she was not ready, they looked in Levey's window at the record covers. Harry came out and told them to clear off! That inspired them to stand with their hands behind their backs and look in more intently than ever, at which Harry got some brown paper and, from the back of the window, covered the contents with it.

Before the CPTA was started, I do not think he had ever spoken to anybody, certainly not to me, but thanks to the half-crown collections, I eventually got on slightly friendlier terms with him and found him to be a man with a logical turn of mind. Harry and his sister were very close and walked through the Passage in the evenings, arms entwined like lovers.

On this particular day, Harry said that he had a problem which he would like to talk to me about.

'I was always under the impression that I owned these two shops,' he told me. 'I thought my father had bought then when he was a young man, but look at this – it's a dilapidations notice. I had a look at the old deeds which I haven't seen for fifty years, and found they were just a ninety-nine year lease, and this lease expires next year! John, I can't afford to do all these things they are asking. What shall I do?'

I could well understand that he could not afford to carry out the dilapidations, for nothing had been done to the premises, except for a coat of paint in response to our scheme, for at least fifty years, and the place was a disaster, inside and out.

'Let me have the notice, Harry and I'll see what I can do,' I said.

Some months before, an estate agency had opened up in Upper Street, in the same block as Levey. It was these people who had delivered the notice. I went to see them. They proved to be a number of college boys, obviously from well-to-do parents who had probably set them up in business to give them something to do. They could not have come down from university very long, as they spoke like adolescents. ('We don't like that word (or that man), do we?' they would ask each other, and agree in a jocularly threatening manner, as if it mattered what they thought). They received me well and I put in a plea on Harry Levey's behalf, stressing that he was an old man, had little money, had thought he owned the place and was suffering from shock at the dilapidations notice. Would they please relent?

They explained that they owned the freehold and that the place was on the verge of falling down. They would like to see him get out. But, I argued, he has lived there all his life and cannot have much longer to live. Our discussion went on for hours, and included a session in the local hostelry to replenish our energies. Finally, they said that would be as kind as they could be, under the circumstances.

I went to see Harry the very next day to relieve his mind. As I walked in, he said:

'John. You look worried.'

'I am worried, Harry,' I answered.

'I'm not!' he said. 'Listen. I never worry. I am a Jew. If Hitler had occupied England during the war, he would have done away with the likes of me. So I have been living on borrowed time ever since, and I don't worry about anything!'

I almost gave up . . .

Harry managed to stay there for quite a few more years. He rented one of the shops to a coin dealer, gave up gramophone records, and concentrated on the sewing machines. He died in 1982. The college boys made their move, and the premises are now very respectable, as are the refurbished and highly-coveted flats above the shops. Everything comes right if you wait long enough.

7

The early months of 1961 produced an enormous demand for shops. The Pierrepont Arcade was fully let, and I was being visited by interested prospective tenants almost every day. I started to look around to see where some more premises could be obtained, and managed to take a number of important steps forward.

I decided to venture into the domain of our Polish friend who had let the boarded-up shop portion of No. 11 Camden Passage to an old chap, who was happy to put up with the Spartan conditions as long as the rent remained extremely low for this 'bed-sit'. Thus I came to meet and know Mr & Mrs Korzeniowsky. I learned that he had escaped to England after the fall of Poland, had joined the Free Polish forces and had been sent to serve with the Royal Air Force. He was a very genuine man, and quite likeable. He had, unfortunately, learnt his English from fellow aircraftsmen at Biggin Hill, and they seem to have taught him only the worst swearwords in the Anglo-Saxon language, so that almost every word was an expletive, each competing with the last for the title of being the foulest. All his conversations were delivered in the friendliest possible manner, which made the swearing more ludicrous than ever. Korzeniowsky had married a very nice, mild-mannered English rose of a woman. She had, by the time I met them, become used to her husband carrying on a conversation in foul English, and occasionally interjected during a particularly flowery flow with 'Oh! Stanislau!'

My diplomatic approaches, asking him to consider throwing out his tenant from the shop and letting it to a shopkeeper, proved to be quite futile. I spent many a pleasant evening with the Korzeniowsky's discussing, when I could, the advantages of a shop tenant over the dirty old man who was there, but the ultimate answer was always 'Not ******* ******* likely!' But even the toughest Pole has his weak spot, and when I was approached by a very high-class lady antique dealer, Kay Kleinfeldt, wanting to buy some shop premises in Camden Passage, I put her in touch with our Polish friend. She must have weathered the language barrier very well and charmed him, for she emerged as the owner of the freehold and Korzeniowsky moved out into the country to grow ***** potatoes and keep ***** chickens!

Kay Kleinfeldt, the new owner of Number 11, was an expert on porcelain and glass. She opened a lovely shop which she called 'The Canterbury', but it was unfortunately a little too early and too up-market for Camden Passage at that stage, and she eventually decided to close down and take a position with one of the leading auction houses in an advisory capacity. This lady told me why she called her shop 'The Canterbury. She was viewing a sale at one of the auction rooms and was looking at a very nice Georgian canterbury when she noticed that there must have been a secret compartment somewhere, as the drawer was not as long as the canterbury was deep. She also felt that it was rather heavier than it should have been, and noticed that it rattled when shaken. She did not pursue the matter in case others noticed, but she managed to buy the canterbury at the auction. When she took it home, she soon found the well-concealed compartment and was delighted to find that it contained some fine Georgian jewellery. It was with the capital acquired by the sale of this jewellery that she bought and opened her shop. It is a pity that she lost some of her capital in the shop, but she never complained.

The first restaurant to open in Camden Passage was 'Portofino'. This now rates in the absolute top class, but it was not always so before Aquilino Consigli took it over from the man who first opened it.

I was visited by a young Italian, Dimarti, who told me he had been working in the West End of London as a waiter, but had now taken a lease on No. 41 Camden Passage and was going to open a restaurant to be called 'Portofino'.

He first needed to get the premises in order – kitchen installed, the place decorated, table and chairs purchased, Chianti bottles hanging on draped fishing netting and so forth.

'I have a marvellous cordon bleu chef, one of the best there is,' he told me. I promised him all the help I could manage, and in due course volunteered to type his menus, from which 'Pollo alla Cacchiatori' still brings back memories of ploughing through the boring task.

The first meal we had there proved to be most disappointing, and I wondered whether I had been guilty of a degree of deception in the glowing press releases I had sent out, proclaiming the advent of a cordon bleu restaurant. However, in the spirit of cooperation, we persisted and took many friends along, but there was no doubt that things were not what they should have been.

Perry Guinness was also doing his utmost, and in that vein took along a high-ranking titled friend, to introduce him to this new restaurant so that he would recommend it to his friends. He was shown to a quiet side table under the dangling chianti bottles and fishermens' nets which, in the purposely dimly-lit restaurant, gave a degree of seclusion. The meal was just passable, but was disturbed by a party of young locals who made a noisy entrance, were given a table and proceeded to be as objectionable as possible, testing the patience of the owner. After some time, having eaten their meal, they got up to leave without paying, saying that they were not satisfied with the meal. There followed a very noisy rumpus between the owner, who was demanding his money, and the locals, who were threatening to give him a hiding if he did not remove himself from the position he had adopted – his back to the front door with arms akimbo to prevent them departing without first parting with some money. The evening was finally spoiled (or was it made?) for Perry and his noble friend when the cordon bleu chef appeared from the kitchen at the rear of the shop, much in the manner of the inevitable cavalry that always appears over the hill in Western movies, wielding a large chopper. I cannot recall what the outcome was, but I suspect that the locals won the day.

The combination of mediocre food and this sort of

trouble could only result in failure, and that is what happened. Just in time the present owner, Aquilino Consigli, appeared on the scene and bought out Dimarti. From that moment on, the restaurant improved dramatically, and has continued to do so ever since until it has reached its present unsurpassable standard.

I am sure Aquilino will not mind my telling of a further drama, which was to take place about a year later when Dimarti reappeared on Aquilino's doorstep and reminded him that when he had sold out to him, he, Aquilino, had said he could only give him a certain sum for the business, but that if he did well, he would give him more. Dimarti had come to collect, having shrewdly waited until he saw Aquilino was doing well. As a result, I was visited by a distressed Aquilino who asked if I could help him. I sent him down to my solicitor, Robert Fawssett of Biddle & Co, from whose office is a very fine view of St Paul's Cathedral. Robert later telephoned me to say that the best way to handle this was for me to act as an intermediary and bring about a settlement between them. It was his opinion that Aquilino had made this promise and was therefore vulnerable.

I made a time for them both to arrive at my home at 106 High Street. I had typed up a letter which said that 'in consideration of the sum of £... (left open), Dimarti relinquished all further claims against Aquilino', and I had this in my pocket. They both turned up, and I asked Aquilino to step inside while Dimarti waited outside in the street.

'As you know, my solicitor says you are going to have to pay up,' I told Aquilino. He reluctantly agreed to negotiate. I went outside.

'Aquilino says he owes you nothing, but how much will you settle for, once and for all?' I asked.

'X amount, and not a penny less,' he answered. I went inside.

'He demands X,' I told Aquilino, who responded in true Italian style, declaring that he owed him nothing but would give him one half of X, but only out of the goodness of his heart. I went outside and made the half-X offer. A great drama ensued for some minutes, culminating in Dimarti declaring that, against his better judgement and at great personal sacrifice, he would accept three-quarters of X. A further offer was submitted and finally, after much opening and shutting of my front door, accompanied by tearing of hair and tearful pleading, a figure was accepted. A cheque on the spot from Aquilino against the signed filled-in document by Dimarti brought about a final solution to the problem.

The moral of this story is that one should NEVER make this sort of promise but must make a final deal at the very beginning.

It was about this time (late 1961) that I had a visit from two gentlemen who asked me if I could find them premises to start a restaurant, an ambition they had always cherished but never achieved. They were John Carol and Dennis Arundel. John Carol had been a film-star and stage-actor – a very good-looking man who was then in his fifties. He was to be the chef and run the outfit, whilst Dennis was a sleeping partner. Dennis Arundel enjoyed the reputation of being a highly-respected arts critic, and wrote a column for *The Times*. I promised them I would see what I could do for them.

Number 2 Camden Passage was occupied by a small printer. He was very supportive of the CPTA, but was unable to do anything about opening up his premises as a shop. He had a bad heart, and it was not being improved by having to run up and down stairs all day long, for the equipment was on the ground floor and everything else on the upstairs floor. I asked him if he would consider selling his premises, and suggested to him that he would be better off finding a place all on one level which would not need to be in a shopping precinct. He told me he had been trying to sell for some months, but his asking price of £750 had brought no response at all. I asked him if he would like me to get £1,500 for the premises, and he looked at me with total disbelief. I made one small condition:

'If I get you £1,500, will you donate two and a half per cent to the CPTA funds?' I asked (we were desperately in need of funds). He said he would be more than happy to. I think he thought I was fantasising.

John Carol and Dennis Arundel were both amazed at the

Taking refreshment outside the Camden Head.

Photo by courtesty of Jim Connell.

speed at which premises had been found and were very happy to pay that sum, so the deal was done.

The printer bought a large shed in a backstreet at a very low price and prepared to move out. Once everything was settled and he had received his money, I went and reminded him of the promised donation to the CPTA funds.

'If it was you, John,' he said, 'I would be delighted to give it, but you are too big (!) to take money. But I won't give anything to that crowd of bastards.' He was apparently referring to my esteemed members, with whom he seemed to have picked a quick and convenient quarrel. So the funds remained in a depleted state. But a step forward for Camden Passage had been achieved.

The restaurant, called 'John's Restaurant', was opened some months later and attracted people from all over the world, including many famous film stars from Hollywood.

John Carol had a liking for the brandy bottle and was, on occasions, a little too enthusiastic with it. He was also sure that he was the most important person present, probably a

82

The open air stalls in Camden Passage.

Photo by courtesy of Jim Connell.

legacy from his film-star days. I recall, still with embarrassment, taking a party of nine people there for a meal one
evening. One of my guests was the well-known journalist,
gourmet broadcaster and wine writer Cyril Ray. John came
from the kitchen to take the orders, and I noticed he was
more than a little sloshed. My gourmet friend was not
satisfied with just ordering a certain dish, but requested to
know whether the ingredients were of a certain composi-
tion.

'Mind your own business!' roared John, refusing to
entertain such insubordination. My face was red, but Cyril
took it in good part.

Ill health forced John Carol to give up after some
eighteen months during which time he had been visited by a
lot of famous people – I have mentioned Spencer Churchill,
and it seemed that most of Hollywood's film stars seemed
to turn up.

The restaurant was then taken over by the famous Robert
Carrier, whose cookery books enjoy worldwide sales. I

83

suppose many of the diners went along to see if Carrier could produce the same mouthwatering dishes that were portrayed in his books. They were not disappointed as long as Carrier was in charge, but I know he sometimes had problems when he was absent for long periods while he was overseas promoting his publications.

Guy des Rochers, who you will remember took the shop at 120 Islington High Street for twenty-five shillings a week, came to me and in his charming French accent said:

'Mr Payton, you ave been very lercky for me and I ave done very well in my shop. I would like to ave more room, and I would like to ask you to try to help me rent nermber 118, next door to me.'

118 High Street had been a herbalist shop for a number of years prior to the war, and was noted for its sign in the window which said something to the effect that many a person had died not knowing that close to their coffin there existed a herb which could have saved their life. However, in due course the owner either failed to look for the correct herb in close proximity or died of natural causes, and the shop became vacant. It was owned by the Circle Furnishing Company, which had its large retail premises in Upper Street where now exists a restaurant, next to Barclays Bank's Islington Green branch. The owner, Mr Freedman, could find no tenant for the High Street shop, so he used it to store the trade-ins he was forced on occasions to accept in order to sell his suites of furniture. The shop was stacked floor to ceiling with old furniture. It was never open as a shop, and was an eyesore. In the flat above lived a lady whose only claim to fame that I can remember was her ability to throttle chickens when asked by my mother during the war, when everyone tried to produce their own eggs to help the war effort.

'Come with me,' I said to Guy, 'and I'll take you to see Mr Freedman.' Guy was a very shy person, and recoiled rather at this meeting being thrust upon him. We walked along to Circle Furnishing and I introduced Guy to Mr Freedman.

'Guy has got the shop next to yours and would like to expand into it, if you could manage it,' I told him.

'Well,' said Mr F. 'I will sell it, but only if I can get £2,000!'

We were both rather taken aback, as it had not occurred to us that the property would be for sale – we were thinking that Guy might get a lease.

Guy then responded as, perhaps, only a good antique dealer can. He rapidly pulled himself together and said:

'I will geev you seventeen undred and feefty.'

'No,' responded Freedman, 'I think two thousand is quite fair, so you think about it and let me know.'

We left the shop and had gone no more than fifty yards when Guy stopped and said, most earnestly:

'Mr Payton, plees do nert tell amywern about thees – plees prermiss me!'

There are those to whom I have related this tale who have said that I should have gone back and bought it myself, but that was not my style.

That is how Guy came to own No. 118 High Street. He did extremely well, and some time later bought out Alfred Geere, his neighbour at 116. He then tore the two premises down and made one magnificent shop in which he stocked some priceless antiques.

To return for a moment to Alf Geere.

Mr Geere's father had been in those premises since the First World War, and in the mid-1920s was the local expert in the radio sets which were just coming into fashion, superseding the crystal sets which had demanded that there be complete silence and, no-one breathe, lest the probe slip from its position on the crystal and the signal be lost. My father bought one of the new radios which did not require a crystal. It revolved on a base and required a long aerial. This was stretched the length of the back garden. There was some sort of switch, set on the wall some way along the garden, which could isolate the aerial from the set – possibly a safeguard against lightning. Once, when the radio went wrong, Mr Geere was called in. He brought with him a meter which consisted of a probe and a wander lead with a spike on the end. He put the spike into one hole at the back of the set and did a spot of probing with the wander lead, while I, all of five years old, watched in awe and admiration. When my father and Mr Geere left the room to go and examine the aerial switch, I childlike, tried my hand at doing exactly what Mr Geere had been doing.

There was a great flash which, according to the two angry men who returned to the scene at the double, could have resulted in the early demise of Mr Geere. In fact, he managed to survive until the late 1930s, when his son Alf took over.

Alf's speciality was bicycle repairs, for which he charged pathetically petty fees. His shop was unkempt. The counter had a couple of racks of records (the old wind-up gramophone type) but I never found out why, as he certainly did not sell records. He did put new springs into the old wind-up gramophones – a task fraught with danger if you failed to keep a firm grip on the coiled spring after the wire which restrained the spring had been removed, for there was great power in those springs which, once released, would fill a room with blue steel coils. He also sold torch batteries and bulbs, and a few other odds and ends. He had an army of children who seemed to live noisily with their mother, who sang happily in the room at the back of the shop – there seemed always to be a baby bawling in the background which Alf seemed not to notice, and he remained quite unperturbed even when the tribe burst out of the room and swarmed all over the shop, counter and all, regardless of whether there was anyone in the shop or not. When the painting scheme was 'on', Alf was the one who painted his shop a bright orange, destroying any hope of a blended colour scheme. Alf Geere was one of nature's gentlemen, and I was pleased to see him get the princely sum of £8,500 for his shop from Guy, only a few years after 118 had been worth only £2,000. He moved into the country somewhere along the Thames, and I think he enjoyed a new way of life – I sincerely hope so.

Guy told me so often how thankful he was to me for the luck I brought to him and for the free service I had given him. It came as a great shock, then, when he and his Irish companion deliberately tried to close down our music school. They were right next door to it and had built a back extension – with my cooperation – which gave them a commanding position to play radios and records at full blast and shout abuse so loudly that the lessons had to stop. I realized they had over-imbibed, but it provided me with one of the greatest disappointments I have ever had. It

Pierrepont Row, Islington Green.

F. N. Shepherd.

shook my faith in 'woman-haters', and I still shudder at the memory of those awful evenings.

☆   ☆   ☆

Then, in 1961, there was Pierrepont Row to consider.

Pierrepont Row consisted of a row of six derelict cottages which had a demolition order on them as dangerous structures. These were small terraced work houses, built in the early 1700s and consisting of two rooms on the ground floor and two upstairs, the front door opening directly into the front room. They were built, no doubt, to house farm labourers employed by the local squire. These farm workers would have been paid very little and expected to work long hours. I have only two memories of them – one from my childhood when my brother showed his prowess on a number of occasions by practically proving that he could throw a stone from No.112 straight through the window of

87

these cottages – resulting in an angry tenant, shouting abuse and threats, presenting himself to my parents who were busily serving in the music shop. The other was in 1940, when an incendiary bomb set fire to one of them. There was deep snow on the ground. We called the fire brigade, but in the meantime tried to contain the fire (with no success) using one of the hand-pumps issued to the local fire-watch brigade. This pump required a bucket of water, one person to pump like fury and another to direct the hose. The firemen arrived and one stood on the wall, and I found I was spraying him. I asked him if what I was doing was any help, and he said, 'No, but keep going.'

These houses were still occupied by tenants paying pittances of rents well into the 1950s, until Islington Council declared that they were uninhabitable and slapped a demolition order on them. The freeholder of these houses had bought the whole lot for a very small sum and, as there was no incentive to go to the expense of knocking them down, there being no interest in the area at all, he had so far failed to carry out the order. Up to the time of starting the rebirth of Camden Passage, the only hope he had was for Islington Council to make a compulsory purchase order, when he would have received very little. It seemed to me that I could do something with this land.

Some enquiries via the rating office showed that a firm of solicitors in the West End of London were responsible for Pierrepont Row. I made a telephone call to the solicitor, Mr Asher Oldschool, telling him I was interested in doing something about the site, and fixed up an appointment to see him the next day.

It must have been manna from heaven for Mr Oldschool – who turned out to be the solicitor for a Trust which owned Pierrepont Row – to have someone showing some interest in what had been, up to that moment, an embarrassing nuisance. I do not think that was the reason that I received a friendly welcome – that has proved to be his nature – but I am sure it helped a little.

I outlined to Mr Oldschool what had happened so far in Camden Passage, and found he was slightly aware that he had seen something about it, but had not connected it with the derelict property now in question. He liked what he heard, and asked what plans I had. I vaguely outlined a development of shops, but at that time had no specific plan in mind. Mr O said he would be most interested to come up to Camden Passage and have a look around, and it was arranged that he would come the following day.

When he arrived we took a walk along Camden Passage and a look at Pierrepont Row – the first time he had seen it. It seems the client for whom he acted was a man who would buy anything as long as it was cheap, and Pierrepont Row had been cheap. I took Mr O to my house, and we sat and had a discussion over a glass of sherry.

The outcome of our discussion was that he was very favourably inclined towards my plans and would strongly recommend them to his client. The atmosphere of Camden Passage has captured many hearts, before and since its rebirth, and I could see that Mr Oldschool was captivated by its charm and possibilities.

A few days later I received a call from him, saying that I should now put forward a definite proposition to him and he was sure it would be acceptable to his client. I was absolutely delighted – this presented a great challenge, as I had never designed a building before.

I had some consultations with antique dealer Leigh Underhill, who was his usual helpful and practical self, and eventually decided that a number of varying sized shops would be the most suitable development, so that stallholders could promote themselves into the smaller units, and I could accommodate some of those established dealers who were looking for shops in the larger units. Out came pencil and paper, and after many hours of planning and then scrapping the plans and drawing up another version, I arrived at what I considered to be the best bet. Sixteen shops of varying sizes with different styles of shopfronts, many with small panes of glass in wooden frames. One essential factor I had to consider was that there should be an easy and natural traffic flow of people through the stalls site and into the arcade of shops, so that anyone taking a shop would never be at a dead end. Also, to provide as much natural light as possible whilst at the same time giving each shop the maximum amount of area possible. Of course, the charming Georgian atmosphere of Camden

Passage must be complemented by the shops.

An overall determination I had was that this arcade of shops would be let to antique dealers only. I do not think there had ever been an arcade built specifically for antique shops – plenty since, but none before. At that time, antiques did not enjoy the popularity that they now have. In the event, as I will relate, I was to allow, after much pleading, a small café to occupy one of the shops, and both the owner of the café and I came to regret this decision.

Someone – I have forgotten who – knew of a quantity surveyor who was good at drawing up plans for submission to the Council. Simon Lack proved to be a very competent, enterprising as well as charming young man – I have never seen him since the job was finished, but did hear that he went to Africa, and I wonder if he ever thinks of the Pierrepont Arcade he put into plan form for me and inspected at each stage of the building – I am sure he must, as it was a very exciting period in both of our lives.

Asher Oldschool liked my plan and promised to grant the project a lease. He also asked how I was going to finance the building. I told him of my strong principle that anything I did in Camden Passage must first be offered to the members of the CPTA, and that I would be making an offer to them all so that they could participate if they wanted.

'If you run short,' said Mr O, 'I have a number of clients who would probably be pleased to put up some cash, so let me know if you need help.'

Our plans were submitted to Islington Council, and it was understood that there would be some two months' delay in that August chamber. By this time, the Council was taking a bit more notice of Camden Passage, although at no time did I find them helpful or even friendly. My 'mole' in the Town Hall would report to me what was *really* going on behind the scenes after my frequent visits to the Town Clerk and the Borough Engineering, and it was not good at all.

Simon Lack submitted the plans to a number of builders and we received some estimates, one of which was accepted. The shopfronts were to be provided separately by an old-established carpentry firm he knew of in Canonbury.

In my innocence, I drew up and distributed to my

members what has since been described as A Prospectus, the purpose of which was to acquaint them with the economics of the building of the Pierrepont Arcade, tell them how much cash was needed, give them my estimate of the amount of rents we might expect to raise when the shops were let, and suggest to them that they might like to put up some money and be a shareholder – I was putting in what I considered to be my fair share of money. I have been told that such a prospectus is frowned upon, and could even have been illegal. Whatever the facts may be, as it was an absolutely above-board document, I suppose it did not matter and nobody came to cart me away. Neither did many of the members seem to think very much of the prospectus OR the prospects, as only two of them responded! After going the rounds of the members again to make sure they knew what it was all about (and being the recipient of the thumbs down from all but the two I have mentioned), I came to the conclusion that I was embarrassing many of them by talking of sums in multiples of £101 (£100 debenture and £1 for a share) as they simply had no money to spare at all. If I have not adequately painted the picture of the state of business in Camden Passage in a previous chapter, I have not done my job properly. There were a few who could have produced some capital (I am sure Danny O'Hara would have, had he been still alive then – but his widow decided against it). It is more than likely that some of the members thought I was going a bit too far with my hare-brained schemes, and could see their money going down the drain if I parted them from it. They were probably bewildered by the speed at which events were happening around them – in the space of a few months, their Passage was transformed from a sleepy back street into a bustling thoroughfare, with outsiders casting covetous looks at their premises.

I had to look a little wider for finance and roped in my then neighbour Don Gurney, the very supportive Cyril Ray and another close friend. That still left me quite a bit short, and I remembered what Asher Oldschool had said about having clients who might be interested. I asked him to see what he could do for me. He came up trumps and was able to promise to provide the balance of cash required.

Everything came together shortly after that – the approval came through from the Council, the lease came through from Oldschool & Co, and we were able to sign a contract with the builders. The starting date was August 1961, and the contract provided for the Arcade to be completed by December 24th of that year.

Once the builders moved in to prepare the site for the concrete raft on which the Arcade was to be built, it is fair to say that chaos existed in that part of Islington High Street which adjoins Camden Passage proper. There is no road access to the Pierrepont Row site. The builder tried to take a lorry along Camden Passage, but was immediately jumped on (literally) by the shopkeepers and quite justifiably so, as all those shops have basements of cellars which extend under the footpath, and there was every chance that a laden lorry could disappear into one of these, there being nothing between the paving stones and the cellars but a few bits of wood and some soil! There was no option for the builder but to carry everything out of the site on wheelbarrows and load it all into a skip parked at the entrance to the Passage, especially as the Council, in answer to complaints about the lorry, put some bollards in so that vehicles could not get through.

The following weeks saw Islington High Street turned into a mudbath once a little rain had fallen (and London can always oblige in that direction). The builders did their best to clean up every evening, but it was a losing battle. But such was the prevailing spirit at that time, there were no complaints and the hardship was accepted cheerfully.

During the excavation of the site, the builders found a sandstone plaque, some eighteen inches square which proclaimed 'Pierrepont Row.1717'. This was in a wall at the end of the gardens belonging to the cottages, and I can only assume that there was a lane at the back instead of gardens when they were first built. We rescued it, and it can be seen set into the wall of the Arcade just by the main gates. The lettering style is charming.

Once the foundations and the drainage system were laid, things went ahead quite well – the bricks which were to be the dividing walls of the shops were laid and the formwork for the flat roof put in place. I recall that the builders had everything ready to pour the concrete for the roof, but required the approval of the local Council building inspector. He came along and condemned their formwork, saying that the strengthening metal must be raised to a certain distance from the top of the concrete. The builders were most depressed by this, and confided in me that the inspector was a fool and did not know what he was talking about. But they had to comply, and they made a load of small supports which met with the inspector's approval. In retrospect, and having since seen other jobs of this nature, I realize that the inspector was quite correct and it was the builder's inexperience that was at fault. Without the inspector's intervention, it is possible that the roof would have cracked up and caved in before many years passed!

The concrete roof was poured in early December, and all that remained for the builder to do was to have it sealed with a bitumen solution and then finish off the rough surface of the concrete footpaths and shop floors with screed. A little bit of bad weather was experienced in early December, and that, coupled with the delay caused by the building inspector, brought us to the deadline for the finished job, and still the screed had not been done. The builder came to me and asked for an extension of time of just one week, without penalty, by which time he would be completely finished. I happily acceded to his request.

On Christmas Day, 1961, London experienced a very severe frost. This frost lasted for three months, and the temperature rose above freezing only a few times and then only for a few hours. Every time our builders floated the screed of cement, it froze, only to break up as the temperature rose above freezing for an hour or two during the day and it defrosted. It was to be the end of March before the Arcade was finished. As all the other jobs the builder had were outdoor work, sadly, he eventually went broke.

Some form of gates would be essential for security. Once again, a few enquiries elicited that there was an antique dealer in Winchester, Hampshire, who specialized in iron gates and other garden furniture and ornaments. I went down to see this character, and he showed me a delightful pair of Georgian gates, very grand and fit for a palace, and just about good enough for our Arcade! I bought them and had them installed in the spot where they are still – and jolly nice they look, too.

The shopfronts were in place, unaffected by severe weather, but the Arcade, scheduled for occupation on January 1st, was not fully ready until 1st April, 1962. I had let only a few of the shops before the end of 1961, but a couple of the tenants were desperate to get into their shop. One was the silver dealer, John Laurie – he is still an important part of the Passage and is now on the corner of Camden Passage and Upper Street – and the other was the only non-antique dealer who I have already mentioned. This was to be a café at No.11 which had extra work to be done to it as it required a water supply and extra drainage. Selwyn, the proprietor, moved in on January 1st. He was surrounded by snow; the path to his shop, had he been able to see it under the ice, was unfinished and what is more, the desperately cold weather kept the public away. I told him that we would not charge him any rent for the first three months, but even so, he was in a desperate state. He came to regard me, helped by some judicious stirring from a few people who had little else to do but drink coffee and feed his worries and who were probably a little jealous of what was being done, as some sort of ogre, and I had quite an unpleasant time with him. I realized he was in a highly excitable state due to the paucity of business, but there was nothing I could do about it, except let him have his shop rent-free and buy a coffee and cakes whenever I could! After a time, I could not even patronize his shop, as he shouted at me and waved his fist every time he saw me! In the course of time, he moved out of the Arcade into another shop and we got back onto speaking, even quite friendly, terms. Time heals. . . .

The shop that Selwyn moved into solved another of the problems for me. The little shop at 13 Camden Passage was occupied by one David Smith, an upholsterer. It was David who vowed, when the painting was going on, that if we dared to touch his shop (we offered to paint it for nothing) he would put excrement all over his windows. There are those who might think this to be unfriendly in the extreme, but I think he was slightly eccentric and definitely ultra-stubborn. I felt we were stuck with this problem for evermore, but to my amazement, one day Selwyn announced that he was moving out of the Pierrepont Arcade as he had bought 13 CP from David Smith! How he managed it I cannot imagine. Perhaps the fact that they were both of the Jewish persuasion may have helped.

In due course, Selwyn set up No.13 as a café, and our Arcade was back to where it should have been in the first place – all antiques.

Once the weather improved, all the shops were leased in a very short time. It was, and still is, my policy to charge as low rentals as possible. One of the reasons underlying the great success of Camden Passage has been the attitude of stallholders and shopkeepers, who are able to be pleasant and happy people because they can easily make profits after paying their rents. Good business is where everyone makes a profit, and those early dealers who took shops were taking a chance on and contributing to the continued progress of Camden Passage.

Even at the very benevolent rents, the Arcade managed to pay off the debt to its shareholders in two years and pay some handsome dividends. Those brave members and friends who took up my original offer have done extremely well out of their investment, and will continue to do so *ad infinitum*.

My shareholders were not the only ones to benefit. The seven-year leases we gave to the antique dealers proved to be highly saleable – the leases allowed them to sell, the only restriction being that the incoming tenant was an antique dealer and was acceptable. Within a very short time, many of the shops changed hands, with astonishingly high prices being paid for these leases. A couple of the shareholders expressed some dismay that the leases were fetching more than they would get in dividends in a few years, but I took the view – and do still – that any dealer who is willing to pay a high premium for a shop in Camden Passage will add something to the Passage. This has proved to be the case.

The rents charged in the Arcade are still comparatively low, although they have had to rise quite significantly over the years. In one way this has acted against the best interests of Camden Passage, in that many of the shops were open for only two or three days a week, presumably

A busy day in the heart of Camden Passage.
Note Finbar MacDonell's print shop on the left.

because they make whatever money they need on those few days. The only alternative would be to charge very high rents so that the tenants need to open for at least five days a week in order to make a living, and this is not an option I would like to consider. Let us hope this is a problem that will cure itself in the course of time.

We live in a world of greedy landlords – particularly in Australia where I now live, where small shops which, as far as position and potential goes, do not start to compare with Camden Passage which is visited by the world, command rents five to ten times our Pierrepont Arcade rents and, what is more, the lease agreements often allow the landlord to take a share of the lessee's profit!

Many of the small shopkeepers who were original members of the CPTA seized the opportunity to let their shops at a good rent or sell them for a good price. Some interesting characters were moving in.

Perry Guinness saw to it that any newsworthy character

Saturday crowds seek out the many bargains on the stalls in front of the Pierrepont Arcade. There are two main market days – Wednesday, the trade day, when a very early rise is advisable and Saturday, which starts at the more civilized hour of 9 am.

who joined the Passage was fully interrogated and used for publicity. One such newcomer in late 1960, was Christopher Gibbs, who took over a small shop at 43 Camden Passage. Under cross-examination, he had to confess to being the son of Sir Humphrey Gibbs, the British Ambassador to America and nephew of Lord Aldenham. Having been reared in opulent surroundings, saturated in antiques, it is little wonder that Christopher became a very talented antique dealer. When we learned that he had an assistant in the shop, Jane Ormsby-Gore, herself high in the social circle, another tit-bit for the William Hickey and similar columns was created.

When, on December 12th, 1960, Christopher Gibbs decided to throw a party in Camden Passage, he could find only one place large enough to hold it – in a then-empty barn-like place at the bottom of Pierrepont Row (now the

Flea Market built up to two floors). This place consisted of a couple of largish rooms leading one into the other. It was probably a cowshed in the early nineteenth century, and was little better in 1960. There were no lights, so candles were placed every few feet around the wall on a convenient shelf.

The night was freezing cold. I had arranged, at Christopher's request, for a French-style accordionist to play on the stall site at the top of Pierrepont Row, and he served also as a guide to where the event was taking place.

The venue soon became very crowded with young socialites including the lovely Gloria Ashley, Lord Christopher Thynne, Lucinda Lambton and the Marchioness of Londonderry, and the drinks flowed freely. There was a distinct smell of 'pot' in the air, and everyone was having a marvellous time. I was told that Prince William was present, but did not see him in the crowd. What I did become acutely conscious of was that the one and only toilet in the place did not work, but seemed to be pressed into service quite often, with the result that it became quite wet underfoot. That seemed not to worry anyone, and the night was a great success.

I made an arrangement with a local photographer, Joe Bulaitis, to be available to pop across the road from his Upper Street shop if we telephoned him to say that there was a celebrity in the Passage. He got many opportunities to place his photographs with the Press, but perhaps his best took place when the word came to me by bush telegraph that the Queen Mother, having visited Robert Carrier's restaurant, following which she went into the print shop of the wonderful character Finbar MacDonnell, was walking around in the Passage. Joe was quick off the mark, but the Queen Mother had gone into Big Chief I-Spy's shop at No.16 by the time he arrived. Camden Passage was very quiet at the time. John hid his camera under his coat and waited until the lovely lady left the shop, having had a long talk with Big Chief Arnold Cawthrow. John got a fine picture, which he placed with the *Sunday Express*.

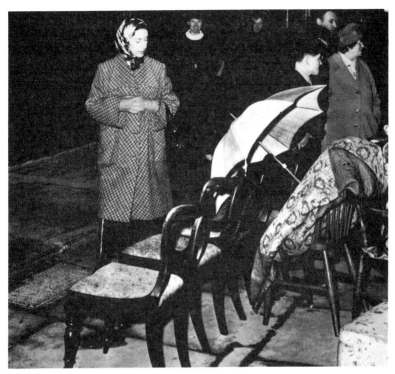

Princess Margaret casts a professional-looking eye
over the offerings in Camden Passage.

Arnold was thrilled at having such an important visitor, and reported that she was delightful and interested in his varied stock. Amongst his stock was an old china chamber pot, and Queen Elizabeth asked if there was much sale for them. When Arnold told her that they were being used as punch bowls, she said: 'Now you are going too far!'

One Saturday in 1964, Princess Margaret and Lord Snowden quietly turned up and spent a long time in the shops and at the stalls, going almost completely unnoticed – but not unnoticed enough for John Bulaitis not to be summoned and for much of the Press to carry a story the next day. Lord Snowden was particularly interested to meet one of the shopkeepers, Eric Thompson, with whom he had been connected in the revue 'Cranks' some years previously.

Camden Passage is a magnet for celebrities and film

stars. Not only as visitors, either. Many television actors and actresses have taken stalls and shops. The star of 'Dangerous Moonlight', the handsome Derik de Marney was observed carting cartons of antiques to a friend's stall. Half of Hollywood's film stars have visited Camden Passage and its superb restaurants.

I should not tell this story as it has an unsatisfactory ending. One quiet day two ladies came into my antique shop, interested in something I had on show. One of these ladies was so beautiful, so perfectly groomed, so expensively and perfectly dressed and exuding such an aura that I would have happily given her anything she asked. The lady with her was obviously her companion. I was too tongue-tied to ask who she was, and I still do not know. A princess? Not a film-star. I wish I knew . . .

8

Alexander Cruden is a name that is known to every churchman in the English-speaking world. Cruden was born in Aberdeen in 1699, and was educated at Marischal College. He came to London as a tutor in 1719. The story has it that he was driven mad by a failed love affair (many of us are driven mad when they succeed). He opened a bookshop in the Royal Exchange, and eventually enjoyed the title of Bookseller to Queen Caroline. It is said that at one time he was a Baptist Minister, and it was this calling that opened his eyes to the fact that there was no reference book, or concordance to the Holy Bible. He therefore set about tackling that seemingly impossible task while he ran his bookshop. He eventually compiled the Complete Concordance to the Old and New Testaments, which entailed making a reference book of every word in the Bible – some 225,000 references. The importance to anyone who is composing a sermon is obvious.

As it was in the early eighteenth century that Cruden was setting about his mammoth task, the reader will appreciate the difficulties he faced. He had no money, and had to rely on getting sponsorship from nobility. This was no easy matter, and was a degrading task to a man with such a noble objective in mind. It made the wretched man quite eccentric, some said a little mad. Those who said he was a little mad got him incarcerated in the lunatic asylum on a few occasions. Once in, it was difficult to get out (still is, I think).

A number of letters written by Cruden to various nobles are in the British Museum library. I was greatly impressed by the efficiency of that organization when I got a student's

ALEXANDER
· CRUDEN ·
DIED IN CAMDEN PASSAGE
1701   1770

Alexander Cruden looks down in the Camden Passage
he knew more than 200 years ago.

The unveiling of the Cruden Memorial plaque by Poet
Laureate, John Betjeman and Church Dignitaries.

pass and asked to see the Cruden letter to Princess
Charlotte. This actual original letter was in front of me
within ten minutes. Written in humble and begging terms,
it asked her to sponsor him (to which she agreed). He
settled down to work with will. After suffering a further
great hardship, he eventually managed to get his master-
piece (for such it was) finished. It took him from 1732 to
1736, and won him special honours at the universities of
Oxford and Cambridge. It was during this period that he
also ran his bookshop. But the Queen inconveniently and
selfishly died just a few weeks after he had finished his
Concordance, which he dedicated to her, leaving him
sponsorless and penniless, a state of affairs which earned
him another session in the asylum (and who can blame
him?). From this incarceration, he removed himself by
cutting his chains.

Cruden lived in Islington for much of his life, and became
known locally as quite a crank. He appointed himself

103

'Alexander the Correcter' – of morals, and trotted around the streets of Islington holding a wet sponge with which he erased any obscene notices he found scribbled on the walls. He broke up street fights whenever he came across them. He would still be in demand in the present times. He even asked Parliament to appoint him 'Correcter to the Nation' but, with their inevitable lack of vision, they refused.

It was John Friend who, in 1964, discovered that for many years and up to his death in 1770, Cruden had lived in Camden Passage. We carried out a lot of research at the British Museum library and the Islington Central Library in Holloway Road, which has a wealth of information about Islington. Included in their treasures was a lithographic portrait of Cruden. A memorial plaque was definitely indicated.

Nearly 200 years had passed since the compiler of this great work had died, and not one commemorative plaque had been erected in his memory. It was up to the Camden Passage Traders Association to rectify this omission. They may or may not be a particularly holy lot, but they could recognize a great man when they saw one – especially if he lived in Camden Passage and was publicity-worthy.

The idea of employing a sculptor to create a portrait plaque was out of the financial question, but I managed to do my first bit of sculpting (using a large meat plate as a template, a packet of clay from the art shop and a knife and fork), based on the library's portrait. Once the bas-relief portrait was finished, I surrounded it with laurel leaves (making plaster mould of leaf and then churning out the leaves one at a time in clay), it looked perfectly adequate and I had it cast in *ciment fondu* with a bronze finish. This was carried out by Angello (of the long noble name), as was the descriptive plaque which is beneath the portrait.

The exact location of the house where Cruden lived was rather difficult, as we only knew that it was 'round the corner from Camden Walk, in Camden Passage'. We had a strong feeling that his dwellings must have been above where the 'Portofino' restaurant now is. We approached Aquilino, the owner, to ask his consent to us installing the plaque on the wall between his two shops. Aquilino was quite agreeable to this until he saw the notice 'Alexander

Cruden. Died in Camden Passage in 1770'. Then he did not like the idea at all – perhaps he was a little superstitious about it, and who can blame him? However, the owner of the property two shops closer to Camden Walk (number 45) was quite pleased to accommodate our plaque, and it was there that we arranged to have it installed when we were ready. The installation of a plaque depicting a man with such strong religious connections called for the arrangement of a very special unveiling ceremony. The holy side of my family is my cousin, Canon Arthur Payton, and it was to him I appealed for help with the planning and arrangements, to which he responded with his usual generosity.

Another ecclesiastic friend was The Reverend Dr Wallbank, rector of that wonderful Norman church near the Smithfield market – St Bartholomew the Great, built in 1123. If the readers have not yet visited St Bart's, they will be delighted if they now do so. I had been in the choir at that church between the ages of ten and twelve, but only on sufferance, because my brother had a superb soprano voice and my mother told the choirmaster it was both of us or neither. When my brother's voice broke, that was the end of my singing career.

When I told Dr Wallbank what was going on about Alexander Cruden, he suggested that I should approach John Betjeman, the Poet Laureate. John Betjeman had his town flat in ancient narrow Cloth Fair, right opposite the church and churchyard where occasionally the Queen distributes Maundy Money to the poor of the Parish. Dr Wallbank gave me Betjeman's address, and I wrote to him.

Yes, came the response, he would be delighted to unveil the plaque to such a worthy man. A date and time were arranged, a month hence. The Rev. D. E. Nineham, Professor of Divinity at the University of London, agreed to carry out the service to bless the plaque.

This called for another reception at 106 High Street. My cousin sent out the invitations to the churchmen including, of course, the very important Vicar of Islington. At the same time, one of my stallholders, through her connections, arranged for some madrigal singers from the Royal College of Music to attend.

☆   ☆   ☆

The pleasant task of picking up John Betjeman from Cloth Fair was volunteered by Perry Guinness, and he later told me what had happened.

He knocked on the door and heard footsteps scurrying down the stairs. John Betjeman opened the door and asked him to come into the hall and wait a few minutes as he had a letter to post. He went upstairs again, and then reappeared with a letter which he put on the hall table. He picked up a rubber stamp which he impressed on the envelope, then licked and attached a stamp. Perry asked what was the significance of all this?

'Every year, I send £10 to the Isle of Man post office and buy stamps. I think they are charming. I use them on my letters. So that people will not miss them, I put a message on my letters, see – 'Note the Charming Manx Stamp'.'

They arrived at 106 High Street half an hour before the ceremony was due to start, John Betjeman in a very worn overcoat, patched at the elbows and held together by a safety-pin.

'I am afraid I am a little rusty on Cruden,' said JB in his inimitable manner, 'I am sure you have all his details, so I would like to borrow them. Do you have a quiet room where I can concentrate – a bedroom will do?'

I installed him in one of my daughters' rooms which had a desk and left him there. Karen my daughter did not know he was in there when she came home a short time later. She went into her room, and was both surprised and pleased to see who was the occupant. When he was assured that she was not inconvenienced by his presence, he said:

'You will be able to tell your children in years to come that the Poet Laureate sat at this desk.' All these years later, Karen has married and is able to do just that.

As we walked from the house to the scene of the ceremony, I got a glimpse of how John Betjeman (sadly, now the late Sir John Betjeman) gathered the material for his poems. In the short 200 yards, he pointed out to me various features which, having lived there all my life, I had never appreciated or even seen. Doors, windows and chimneypots attracted his attention, and the crescented Charlton Place gave him a lot of pleasure.

It was a happy ceremony, John Betjeman was besieged by

admirers, many of whom asked if he would come and take a look at their church. Once again I saw the humanity of the great man, for he made notes of all the requests and said he would do his best to come and see them, and I am sure he did.

There left only one duty to perform – to get back to 106 and sample the wine and soft drinks provided. My late brother-in-law, a tall man of dignified stature, had volunteered to be the 'barman', himself being quite interested in a spot of imbibing. He dispensed the drinks, now and then sustaining his energy with one for himself, from the kitchen which was separated from the large room by a sliding door.

I have never seen so many Anglican clergy in one spot – there seemed to be far more than had attended the ceremony! My 'barman' reported that he, too, had not seen booze disappear as fast as on that occasion and, perhaps because he felt there might be none left for his own need, he eventually drew across the sliding door with great dignity, after which there was a general exodus.

Alexander Cruden is still in position in Camden Passage on the wall of No.45. Below his plaque there is a suitable tribute, borrowed from Nelson in 1811, 'Whom neither infirmity nor neglect could debase'.

9

I have mentioned before that Number 1 Camden Passage is situated right opposite 114 Islington High Street. When I was a child, there were two terraced cottages there, numbers 1 and 3, followed by the corner shop (5) and the next one (7), which had been turned into commercial premises by the Warwick Time Stamp Company who were clockmakers and manufactured those machines which employees have to use to mark their card with their time of arrival and departure from work. At Number 1 a poor family lived, the lot of them with ginger hair, but in number 3 there lived a widow, Mrs Tarrant, who spent most of her day gazing out of her first-floor flat window. My brother and I irreverently dubbed her 'Nosey-Parker'. I never heard her talk, but talk she must have as my parents became aware of various antics which took place in our second-floor room, such as when my older brother talked me into trying to descend from the second to first floor via the window, hanging onto a rope which had been lowered, one end tied to the leg of the bed. I never made it, and was hauled back in before my irate mother came to check on her 'information received'. Warwicks incorporated Number 3 into their commercial operation, and we were spied on no more.

To the left of Number 1, there had always been a long blank wall which extended as far as Phelps Cottage and did nothing except provide a back wall to the builders yard which had its frontage in Upper Street. This business stocked everything for use in the interior of a house, including plumbing items, sand and cement. The lavatory bowls and porcelain sinks were stored on the roof of the single-storey shed, and these were part of our everyday view as we looked from our second-floor bedroom over the lavatory bowls to a clear view of the high pavement shops in Upper Street.

In the early hours of a morning in 1959, hearing a crash of glass (a not uncommon sound in those times), I jumped out of bed and noted that the glass was still falling where a brick had been thrown through the shop window of a television/radio shop on the high pavement in Upper Street. The man who had thrown the brick stood on the pavement and waved his arms about a bit before turning and running into a small white van and driving away. This seemed very strange behaviour for an honest-to-goodness smash-and-grab artist. In the morning, I walked across and spoke to the manager who was standing in the window, clearing up the glass.

'Funny business,' I volunteered.

'I wouldn't say it was at all funny,' he answered, 'I lost fourteen television sets and six radios in that smash-and-grab'.

I said no more, but felt it a duty to tell the local CID what I had seen. A plainclothes detective came along and asked to be taken to the bedroom where I saw all this. He cross-questioned me closely and came to a conclusion:

'You would be surprised how long it takes you to wake up and get out of bed,' he said, to my utter astonishment.

'But I saw the glass falling,' I told him.

'Imagination,' was his final verdict. 'We've found the van and there was a television set in it.' I left it at that.

Some weeks later it was found that the manager had been running his own business within his employer's business and selling TV sets on credit. Half the people who were coming to the shop every week were his own 'private' customers! As an auditor was due to visit the branch for a stocktake, the bogus smash-and-grab was arranged in order to account for the shortage of stock. I do not know if they ever caught the manager, but some weeks after the 'event' I saw him furtively peering across at the shop from behind the power station (now The Mall). The police had made it clear to me that it was none of my business, and I let him get on with it.

To get back to the builders yard, the two owners (both CPTA members) decided in 1966 to move to more suitable premises and close down their Islington premises. This left vacant Phelps Cottage and the adjoining shop fronting on Upper Street, together with the builders yard – quite a large area, occupying half the block. Here was another opportunity to satisfy the never-ending demand for shops.

Being an arcade designer from way-back (Pierrepont Arcade), I very soon envisaged and produced a plan which included putting an end to the long life of the plain, boring wall which had presented itself to Camden Passage for the past hundred years or so. As it was a gateway from Upper Street to Camden Passage, that is what I called the arcade. The 'Gateway Arcade' opened up a further twelve shops as well as a large corner shop (which at the time I retained for my own antique business) and two small shops in the lower part of Phelps Cottage.

Just a word about Phelps Cottage. The name Samuel Phelps was carved above the front door, and for as long as I can remember the public in general and locals in particular metaphorically raised their hats as they passed the door, sure in the belief that a famous literary genius had once occupied this charming cottage. Hoping to find a story for some more publicity, we researched Phelps and found that he was no more than a slate merchant – honourable in itself, but not as romantic as it might be. The story of the New River is quite fascinating. This was due to the enterprise of Hugh Myddleton, a very enterprising Welsh-man, born in 1560, who served an apprenticeship as a goldsmith and became a jeweller to the Crown, got into the cloth-making business, had a not very successful stab at mining for coal, and became a Member of Parliament in 1603. A scheme aimed at extending the greatly inadequate supply of fresh water to London had existed for some years, but seemed to lack a person with sufficient tenacity of purpose to embark on it. This is where our Hugh took up the challenge, and he put a plan to the Corporation of London, to bring fresh water from Hertfordshire on a forty-mile route, ending at Clerkenwell where it would be pumped to houses in London. The plans were accepted, and he commenced work in 1609. Nothing much changes, so it is not surprising to learn that he had considerable trouble obtaining permission from land owners and farmers to run the river through their properties, and many a court case was fought before the

110

project was completed. In fact, this led to the project running out of both money and time (a four-year limit had been given), and Hugh had to approach King James I for funds. The king agreed to provide half the funds needed, but on condition that he got half the profits.

To appreciate the enormity of the task, it must be borne in mind that it was essential for the water to maintain a gradual fall of some three inches in a mile. Thus, brick tunnels had to be built through hills and wooden troughs raised on supports to carry the water across the valleys. At last, in September 1613, fresh water reached the New River Head at Clerkenwell, to the accompaniment of much rejoicing and pageantry. As a result of his great achievement, Hugh Myddleton was made a baronet. A statue of Sir Hugh in Elizabethan costume stands at the corner of Islington Green, where Upper Street and Essex Road join. Prior to his enterprise, London's water was dangerous to drink, coming as it did mainly from the Thames which was polluted, serving as a sewer as well as a water supply. Anything resembling fresh water had to be bought from water sellers who carted their supplies from outlying areas such as Highbury, Paddington and Tyburn. The water supply was obviously a contentious issue, and there is a cartoon of the period which shows a tap turned on and frogs and toads coming out of it.

City people would go to Islington, which stood at the top of a long hill, to get some fresh air and fresh water, and Islington became a fashionable place to live for that very reason. Mind you, they had to watch out for their safety whilst making the journey from the City to Islington, as there were countless robbers and highwaymen ready to fleece them. As a result, an armed guard service was set up to safely escort the public to Islington, but even so, travellers from the north preferred to spend a night at the Angel Inn, the Red Lion, or the Crown and Woolpack, rather than risk the final lap to London.

10

For those who are interested in getting into the antique business, either as collectors or dealers, it may be of help to them to explain how I entered that field.

Our music studios were at 114 Islington High Street, and all the upstairs rooms and the back room of the shop were devoted to tuition and practice rooms. The shop was being used as a showroom for an importing business. This, of course, did not agree with what I was preaching – I knew *nothing* about antiques. A little thing like that must not stop the enterprising would-be antique dealer, and I went out and found a few contacts, one of which was a charity organization which collected just about anything anyone would give them. They put leaflets into letter-boxes, saying they would collect any old clothing, bric-a-brac etc, and call a few days later to pick up.

When I called to see these folks, they told me they were well patronized but would put me on a sort of waiting list. I mentioned that I knew quite a bit about violins, and asked if they were ever given any. That struck a chord, if I may make a small pun, and they said that they got quite a lot of violins and it always worried them they may be selling a valuable one at the low price they had put on all violins. I made a proposal that I would vet all their violins in future, if I might get the first look at all the bric-a-brac items. The deal was made and, in the years that followed, a few valuable violins were detected, to the benefit of the charity involved. On the other hand, on one day a week, at the appointed time, a room full of 'junk' was unlocked and I was let loose amongst it all.

At the beginning I did not know what I was looking at and

would chance my arm on the basis that it looked pretty good to me, so someone else may feel that way, too. I would put my selection in a heap in the middle of the floor and the boss would come in and make a price for the lot. I was sometimes quite shocked at the price but rarely said anything, feeling it would all even out in the long run, which it did.

A girl student showed interest in coming along every Saturday to sell the stuff, and I was in the junk business, for as yet I could not glorify the operation as an antique business!

As the weeks went by, I began to appreciate the difference between modern and old, junk and quality. When I picked up my weekly collection, I would put it all in the showroom out of sight after taking out any items I thought were worthy of special investigation. First thing Saturday morning, my student would spread it all out and I would go through and price every piece. A lot would go into boxes which she would label 1/- or 2/6d, and other pieces were individually priced. I still knew not what I was doing. I recall a local dealer coming along and picking up a small bowl from the two-and-sixpenny box. He held it up:

'How much is this?' he asked. I knew that I had made a 'boo-boo', but answered:

"O.K. It's 2/6d provided you tell me what it is.'

He produced his 2/6d and handed it to me:

'Now it's mine, right?' he said. 'This is a Dr Wall Worcester bowl, circa 1765 – it even has the crescent mark underneath.'

Two weeks later, there was a small jug in my weekly collection which I immediately recognized as its brother. I still have it. I suppose it was a small price to pay for education.

My visits to the charity were the highlight of my week, during which my time was fully occupied running my businesses and working for the Passage, so being able to buy a stock in a couple of hours once a week was a blessing. I cannot adequately describe the thrills and education I obtained over the years.

If I had not be fortunate enough to make that contact, I would have spent my time visiting the small antique dealers

ssage Antiques

"and you're quite certain it isn't bent?"

Artist/cartoonist Victoria Davidson sums up one of the dangers of dealing in antiques.

in London and the country, but that would have taken a lot of time which I did not have to spare.

It is worth reminding the reader that interest in antiques in the early 60s was nothing like it is now. In fact, Camden Passage was responsible for a big leap in public interest in seeking and collecting antiques. But in the early 60s people were clearing out all sorts of interesting and valuable items with one thought only – to get them out of the way. Well, I found I gained on the swings what I lost on the round-abouts, and had a very thrilling time in the process. I still have a few items that I bought, thought they were of more than normal interest and took them home to clean up and examine. One such treasure was a clock which was as black as the ace of spades. I took it home and pulled it to pieces and realized that it should have been gold, not black. Some tentative cleaning with weak ammonia revealed some amazing results. The clock was fine ormolu and the face and panels were hand painted Sèvres; the period about

114

1860. Every week found me attacking something with various chemicals, with bated breath.

After some months I was approached by a country antique dealer. He wanted to be able to send in furniture on a 'share-the-profit' basis. He had his eye on our artists' material shop, which was far too large for art alone. I was happy to agree, and that started a business association which was to last for many years to the satisfaction of both parties.

Having entered the antique furniture business, I was encouraged to try to buy some stock of our own. The country house sales I saw advertised looked as if they could be interesting. The trouble was, I had very little spare time. I decided to try to visit one as an experiment. I saw a country house sale that was about a hundred miles from London, and I decided to take the day off and chance my arm. Up at 6 a.m. and out of London before the populace was awake, I arrived at the house at 9 a.m., in plenty of time to have a look around before the sale started at 10.00 a.m.

What an enjoyable and exciting experience that was! At the end of the day I had bought quite a few pieces of furniture, some china, a few bits of silver and a painting or two. There was even a local carrier there who took my order to transport the lot to London. It proved to be a very successful sortie, and laid the pattern for a similar exercise about once a month. On another occasion, I bought a leather-covered, handpainted sedan chair, and this made a good talking point until the display department of Macey's of New York bought is as a decoration.

The sale which I remember most took place in a private house close to the Lords cricket ground. I had seen it advertised, and made a note to go and view it on the day previous to the sale. I had a feeling that this was to be a good sale. On the viewing day, the manager of my antique shop did not show up for work and this confined me to the shop, feeling all the time that I should close it and go to the viewing. However, I did not but determined that, manager or no manager, I was going the following day. I turned up at the same time as the auctioneer's staff and asked if I could have a look around.

'No,' they said, 'you had your chance yesterday.'

The sale was to take place in a very large room – it was a fine house – and items were to be shewn at one of the open doors, across which a table had been placed. I took up my position at that table and I did not move from it all day! The auctioneer's staff brought what items they could to the doorway, but no furniture was displayed at all. I bought all I could see and a few pieces I did not see but took a punt on.

The following day I went along to collect my purchases, and then took a look at what I had been sold. The contents of Bedroom 1 had been knocked down for £35 to a man who was now standing in its midst, looking decidedly dazed. And so he should, as the bed, wardrobe, dressing table with seat to match and two small bedside chests of drawers were of such fine quality that one piece alone was worth many times what he had paid for the lot! A similar situation existed in Bedroom 2, which went for £25. Everything in that house was of superb quality, and it would have been quite safe to buy sight unseen. But I did not know that, thanks to my employee who did not turn up the previous day. Those items I purchased all sold in a flash and at very good profits.

There is no doubt that the antique business is the most interesting and fascinating of all. One has to take chances, but once the eye is experienced, the mistakes become fewer and fewer. There are so many aspects of the trade that one is learning something new all the time.

It was not uncommon to see an item start out on a stall on a Saturday morning, sell to another stall, then another until one of the shops bought it and it probably bounced around the Passage shops, everyone making a small profit, until an outside dealer took it away.

There are some dealers who prefer to specialize, some in a very narrow field. One dealer who had a Gateway Arcade shop for some time gave me a preview before he opened up his shop.

'When is your stock arriving?' I asked, for he had only four pieces on the shelves.

'This is it,' he replied. 'I specialize in ninth and tenth century Japanese pottery, and all of these pieces will be bought by museums.' He told me he knew nothing about anything else. His main difficulty lay in trying to buy at sales. He was one of only a very few dealers who could identify true Japanese pottery of that period, so he was watched carefully at sales to see if he was bidding. Mainly, he had to get a friend to bid for him. But he said that he never had to pay a lot for his purchases and they sold for thousands, but he could go for months without finding anything.

Many of the stallholders asked me whether I thought they should give up their job (as a clerk or shop assistant) and try to become full-time antique dealers. I would always encourage them to do so if they were not married with children. If they were so encumbered, I would suggest to them that they kept going with a stall but ploughed back their profits until they could afford to be more independent.

As for collecting antiques, I can thoroughly recommend it as a most profitable and intriguing pastime, hobby or business.

11

The rating system in London is one which has always caused hardship to small businesses. There are two factors involved. Firstly, the properties are revalued by the Valuation Officer periodically, and they take into account any improvements to the property, any new extensions and so forth. Secondly, a rate-in-the-pound is established annually by the Council and, of course, this goes up every year. The whole thing gets out of hand and very often out of reach of the shopkeeper. I believe that this got to such ridiculous proportions in areas like Bond Street that the rates were more than the rent, and many longstanding businesses were forced out. One such business close to my heart was Hills, the violin experts, who had a lovely old shop in Bond Street that had been there since the seventeenth century and which was mentioned in *Pepys Diary*. They found it necessary to move out of London, and this meant a loss of an irreplacable historical gem to London.

I once had to contact Hills in strange circumstances. The day before Good Friday, a woman came into my music shop and asked if I would like to buy a violin. I said I would like to see it, and she handed me a case. As soon as I opened it, I knew I was in the presence of an Italian master violin, and a glance at the two bows showed they were in the same class.

'How much are you asking for this?' I asked.

'Forty pounds,' the good lady replied, (it was worth fifty times this amount).

'Why are you selling it?' – a leading question.

'It doesn't belong to me,' she replied,'It's my father's. He plays in a band.'

Enough said – it was obviously stolen. Some high-ranking

musician must be mourning its loss. But how to get her to leave it?

'I wonder if you would leave it with me so that I can look up some books,' I said. 'I think it might be worth more than you are asking.'

'I need the money now. I'll take thirty.' Oh! dear, this is difficult.

'No. I could not do that. What about leaving it and coming in tomorrow (Good Friday) – I'll be here, and can then give you what it is worth.'

'I'll take twenty!'

'No. Leave it here and come back tomorrow at about 11 a.m. I insist.'

She had no option. I gave her a receipt and she reluctantly departed.

I telephoned the CID at Islington police station and told them all about it, and asked them to find out who had lost it, as I was sure it was stolen. They phoned me back.

'No. It's not stolen. You can buy it. No violins have been reported stolen.'

'But it *must* be stolen. Please make some more enquiries.'

The detective had had enough of this crank, and made it clear that he did not wish to hear any more from me – he had given me permission to buy it, so get off the line.

I telephoned Scotland Yard and asked for a senior officer. I told him my story, and again emphasised that it *had* to be stolen. The inspector said he would ring me back.

Time went by, and it was late afternoon before he did so.

'It is NOT stolen,' he told me sternly. 'You should have listened to Islington and not wasted my time. I have checked, and there are no violins reported missing.'

'But . . .'

'That is enough.' Reprimanded by no less than Scotland Yard, I cleared the line.

I telephoned Hill & Son in Bond Street. They had closed, but the man I spoke to was working late. He knew nothing of the shop business, but said that Desmond Hill would be at home and gave me his number.

As soon as I started to tell Desmond about the violin and two bows, he was able to tell me that they belonged to one Lionel Monti, professional musician, and that they had been stolen from his car the previous evening and *had* been reported to the police! He suggested I telephone Monti, but had to confess he did not have his new number, Monti having just moved house. I felt sure I would locate it – did I not have the resources of Scotland Yard at my command after the mess they had made so far?

My inspector friend, when I got back to him, had the wind taken out of his sails rather, and was now quite polite.

'Now, please locate Lionel Monti,' I asked, and told him why Hill did not have his number. The Inspector said he would phone me back, which he did after some time.

'Impossible to trace!' he told me. It was now getting quite late.

Out came the telephone directory. There were about thirty Monti's. I ignored those described as butchers, plumbers and so forth, and started telephoning the rest.

'Excuse me. Do you have a Lionel Monti who is a musician?' I asked. No luck with the first three, but the fourth, a teenager, came up trumps:

'Uncle Lionel. Yes, hang on and I'll get his new number.' (It makes me wonder whether those at Scotland Yard are not able to learn from Sherlock Holmes!).

The number produced Mrs Monti, who said her husband had, indeed, lost his violin, but would not be back until very late, as he was recording at the People's Palace, Mile End Road.

I could not wait, so I telephoned People's Palace, who said that Monti was playing and could not be disturbed. I explained the predicament, and asked if they would get him as soon as they could. He rang about an hour later during an interval. I gave him my address, and suggested he should come to me immediately after the concert. He did, wisely bringing a police inspector with him. He was delighted.

'We'll be here to arrest this woman tomorrow,' said the inspector.

'I do not want her arrested on my premises,' I told him. 'I will get her out of the shop, and your people can follow her and pick her up when she is well away from here.' (I was not going to risk having a brick through the window or even on my head). He was not happy about it, but in view of all the bungling they had done so far, he could only agree.

The next morning, two detectives arrived and I told one to go into the cellar directly below the shop where he could hear everything, but not to interfere. The other, to wait further along the street and follow the lady, but not pick her up until she was far from the shop.

She came at 11a.m., and I told her I had found out that this was quite a valuble violin, far beyond my modest means, but that if she took it to my friend , the violin dealer, Withers of Wardour Street, he would be able to buy it. I had an awful job getting her to leave the shop with the violin, but she eventually went.

It was well into the afternoon when I got a call from the police. They had stopped her at Old Street, about a mile away, taken her to the station and got an address from her of her man-friend. They went to the address, but the house was empty. While they waited, a man came along and when he saw the burly cops, he ran like the wind. They chased him, one running, the other in the car, and he travelled a great distance – he was in very good shape, the cop told me – before running into a house. The cops gave chase, through the house, over some walls where one of the police hurt himself, but eventually caught him. Back at the station, the man, a Pole, confessed to stealing the violin from a car, and asked for another ninety offences to be taken into consideration!

Monti got his violin back, and was very grateful. I would not accept a reward, but I suggested he make a donation to the police benevolent fund, which he did not think was very funny or acceptable under the circumstances. He sent me a nice present a few weeks later.

I felt it right to make a complaint to Scotland Yard. The outcome of that was that one day, the shop doorway was darkened by two large gents who announced themselves as Superintendents of police. They said they had come to apologize; they had reprimanded the people in question, particularly the sergeant who had been so rude to me at Islington. Did I want him demoted, they asked me? I declined. You do not often get this sort of sport. I had thoroughly enjoyed myself and would not want to spoil it, but I just hoped the message got across to the police involved.

Dare I mention that an almost identical set of circumstances arose again a couple of years later, when a youth brought in a fine oboe and I had to do all the tracking down, via the maker, a doctor in Wootton-under-Edge in the Cotswolds, whose daughter had left her instrument in the tube train. Again the police were hopeless, one of them telling me that they were allowed to make local calls only!

But back to the Rates!

For many weeks, an official from the Rating Valuation Office had been prowling around Camden Passage – I shall call him Mr Brown for the purpose of this narrative. It was 1963, and Camden Passage was still battling its way uphill. Whilst it was becoming an active antique centre, the ordinary shops were not feeling the benefit. What was he up to? Why was he spending so much time in and out of the shops? Why was he prying into everything? These were the questions being constantly asked by our shopkeeper members.

I began to follow in his tracks and to make notes of what he was saying as he got into long conversations with members. At No.8 Camden Passage, there was a small newsagency-cum-sweetshop run by Mr and Mrs Ruffett. When I went to see Mr Ruffett he was quite irate.

'What right has this Mr Brown to tell me that I should not be in Camden Passage; that I should move out and let an antique dealer in?' he raved at me. 'I'm as entitled to be here as anyone else, and I've been here a long time.'

The same sort of complaint reached me from a number of the original members. I also had a visit from Brown. He waffled on about many things, but seemed to have nothing particular in mind. He did say that he had a relative in the antique business, and I wondered if his visits had anything to do with that connection.

It all became clear on the last day of March 1983, when every shop in Camden Passage and Islington High Street received a notice that the rates on their shops had been *doubled*. In England, the tax year is from April 6th to April 5th. Once we had recovered from the initial shock, it dawned on us that not only had the rates been doubled, but that the increase dated back to the first day of the year! No businessman can operate where he is unable to make a planned budget until *after* the year has ended, but this was the implication of these retrospective rates increases. A foul body blow, indeed.

An emergency meeting of the CPTA was called and battle plans drawn up. All shops were to file a protest and ask for a hearing before an appeal court. I offered to appear on behalf of all of them, and this was accepted. We could not afford lawyers.

We all sent in our objections and awaited developments. In due course, we were advised that our case would be heard at the Rates Appeals Tribunal to be held at the Town Hall.

The interim period had not been wasted. It is possible to obtain information about the rates being charged in Islington at the library, and it was there that I spent a lot of time. It became quite obvious by comparisons that Camden Passage had been singled out for 'milking' by the authorities, no doubt because they had seen all the publicity in the national press and assumed that fortunes were being made and they would like their share.

For the hearing before the Tribunal, I prepared a number of charts as well as many lists of comparisons with other shopping areas of Islington. It was with all this evidence that I turned up at the hearing, supported by a large number of members who sat in two rows behind me.

We were ushered into a hall which was set out as a court. Mr Brown and his outriders had a position directly in front of the raised dais for the judges, while we had a side position to the left of the court. I asked the attendant for a blackboard and easel, for I needed to pin up my charts. He eventually found them and put them to the front of the court near me.

'All stand,' called the clerk.

In came an elderly lady and two elderly gentlemen. No wigs, no gowns. ('Jobs for the boys', I thought, and was not far wrong.)

The old lady took the centre position and indicated to Brown that he should state the Valuation Officer's case, which he did at some length. When he had finished, she looked towards me:

'Now it's your turn,' she said.

123

'I would like to ask Mr Brown some questions,' I requested.

'You can't do that,' she replied,' because if you ask a question, you have to sit down while the Valuation Officer replies, and if you sit down, you can't stand up again.'

Heaven's above! What sort of place is this, I asked myself!

'I am not willing to accept that,' I replied. 'I don't think Mr Brown will mind answering my questions while I remain standing, will you Mr Brown.'

This was not fair, because he could hardly refuse.

'I agree,' he replied.

I asked him a few questions, to which he replied. I then stood on my feet for the next couple of hours, delivering all the evidence I had gathered.

When I was finally finished, relieved looks came over the faces of the three judges, the Chairman (I suppose that was what she was) said they would leave the court to give consideration to the evidence.

A few minutes later they reappeared – 'ALL STAND' – and announced that they would give a five per cent discount off the new rates. I told her that I thought it was disgusting and that we would take our appeal further.

It seemed to me then and it still does now, that the whole thing was a sham and a farce. In fact, it was only a week or two later that I was talking to a taxi driver, and he told me the old lady was a relative of his and that she had no qualifications for the job except that she had given a lot of service to the local Labour Party. That figured . . . Jobs for the boys *and* girls.

The next step was to appeal to Somerset House, and this I did. I eventually appeared before a committee there and submitted all my evidence and pleas. I was told that their verdict would be communicated to me in due course.

About one month later, I received a letter which said that our appeal had been considered, but they would not change the ratings.

I telephoned the man who wrote the letter.

'Did you write that letter?' I asked.

He sounded quite nervous as he admitted it.

'I want another appointment as I don't accept your

verdict,' I told him, with some force.

He arranged then and there for another meeting!

At this meeting, also at Somerset House, I was supported by John Friend of the O'Hara toyshop. I did a lot of drama, using people like Harry Levey as an example of the misery and havoc they were bestowing on my members (of course, this was perfectly true – it was a very severe blow to all of us). But most of all, I told them that I was going to release to the National Press the full story of what had been going on in Camden Passage; of all the peculiar things that Brown had been saying to my members. Put together in the right order, all his comments and hints looked quite sinister. It was quite a wearing performance. I was promised a reply in th course of time.

A few days later, I saw the Chief Rating Officer, Brown's boss, walking up and down High Street.

'I think he wants to bump into me,' I thought. I went out and 'bumped into him'.

'Ah. Mr Payton. I was wanting to talk to you. Would you like to make an appointment? Your place or mine?'

'Yours.' I chose. The following day.

We sat down in his office and did a deal on every one of the premises in contention on the basis of:

'Let's start at No.2 Camden Passage. We say X, what do you say?'

'I say Y.'

'Could we say Z?'

'I would prefer Z -twenty per cent.'

'Agreed! What about No.4?'

That is how we went through the whole of Camden Passage, resulting in a saving of many thousands of pounds to our members and being saved from extinction for many.

I thought at the time it was more like the business methods of Petticoat Lane, but I was willing to deal in any way in order to save Camden Passage being ruined by these officials. Brown was not seen again in Camden Passage, and I suspect he was transferred elsewhere.

12

In 1717, one John Pierrepont took a lease on some land in Islington. What he leased was described as 'that parcel of land including that late Mansion House, now being built in two new messuages or dwellings, with the orchard and gardens thereto belonging, by estimate measuring 274 feet to the road to the West (now Upper Street but then High Street), 100 feet to the North, 224 feet to the East and 100 feet to the South'. All this cost him the sum of £10 per annum.

By the time 1776 arrived (according to another document), Pierrepont had built sixteen messuages or dwellings on the property 'to wit ten in the front or West part and six on the North side together with yards, gardens, ways watercourses, profits, commodities, lights, easements and appurtenances', and his landlord, Gerard Ann Edwards, was making him pay £45 a year for a sixty-one year lease. The payments were covenanted to be paid on the following days: 'the two most usual Feasts or Days of payments of the year (that is to say) the Feast days of the Annunciation of the Blessed Virgin Mary and Saint Michael the Archangel'.

Numbers 100 to 118 Islington High Street are identified as the ten messuages on the west side, and these were called Pierrepont Row up to 1877, and there were six cottages on the north side. These six were those that were condemned and demolished to make way for the Pierrepont Arcade in 1961, but up to 1877 were called Little Pierrepont Row. Numbers 120 and 122 Islington High Street must have been built after 1766 (122 was fire-bombed by Adolf in 1943, which is why it is now a stall-site). However, all these properties were called Pierrepont Row right up until 1877, when they became Islington High Street, and the previous High Street was renamed Upper Street. At some time after 1766, the seven fine Georgian properties which now number 86 to 98 were built and were called Pullens Row. Two of these have since been converted to shops, no doubt at the same time as the rest of the High Street premises were similarly converted.

Now the owner of the land which was leased to John Pierrepont was Gerard Ann Edwards, whose son, Gerard Noel Edwards, was married to the daughter of one Charles Middleton. Middleton was Comptroller of the Navy from 1776 – 1790, and had previously distinguished himself in 1761, when he was commanding the frigate *Emerald* in the West Indies, all of which earned him a Baronetcy on 23rd October, 1781, 'he being of Barham Court and Teston Kent'. He was also a Tory Member of Parliament from 1784–90; a Rear Admiral in 1787 and a Vice Admiral in 1793; then Lord of the Admiralty in 1794/5 and Admiral of the Blue in 1795. In 1805 he was created Baron Barham, 'with special rem of that dignity on default of issue male, to his only daughter and heirs male of her body.' When he died in 1805, he left in his Will £10,000 to each of his fourteen grandchildren. One of these male issue was Sir Charles Noel Noel, who later inherited the title Baron Noel, Viscount Campden, Earl of Gainsborough.

The Islington Central Library in Holloway Road, Islington, has a very extensive collection of documents, pictures and information about old Islington, but they can find nothing about this Mansion House or anything to connect the Gainsborough family with Islington. Yet, at the back of Camden Passage, we find two parallel roads – Gerard Road and Noel Road, both of which are in the area granted to John Pierrepont in 1717. I take a guess that Mansion House prior to 1717 was a country residence of the Gainsborough family.

There were five manors in Islington, each with their Manor Houses – of which the most important were Highbury and Canonbury (the others were Prebend, Barnsbury and St John of Jerusalem). Canonbury House, with part sixteenth century Canonbury Tower, is the only surviving Manor House. Its residents have ranged from Sir

John Spencer, sixteenth century Lord Mayor of London, to the late Sir Basil Spence, the famous architect who designed the new Coventry Cathedal and who was a great supporter of Camden Passage. Highbury Manor was a summer residence of the Prior of the order of St John of Jerusalem, and was destroyed in 1381 during a peasants' revolt which took place under the leadership of Jack Straw (the site continued as Jack Straw's Castle well into the nineteenth century).

Going further back into Islington's history, we find it was called 'Gislandune' prior to 1000 A.D., whilst in the Doomsday Book it is called Isendone, with a population of 210 people. At that time it was farming land and pasturage, most of the land then belonging to the Canonage of St Paul's Cathedral.

It is known that King Henry VIII hunted game in and around Islington, and in true sporting manner decreed in 1546 that none of his subjects were allowed to hunt there (in case they got some of his game). It is more than likely that he stayed in our mysterious Mansion House.

Queen Elizabeth was a frequnt visitor to Islington – she was quite a gal when it came to visiting her richer subjects. Together with her retinue, she would just turn up and expect the treatment to which she was accustomed. It is known that she visited Sir John Spencer at Canonbury House and other Islington residents such as Robert Dudley, Earl of Leicester, and Sir Thomas Fowler, Lord of the Manor of Barnsbury (whose Manor House was in Cross Street). Perhaps she also visited Sir Walter Raleigh who, when a young man, lived in what is now Upper Street. I throw in that she *must* have visited our Mansion House – how could she miss it?

The Queens Head public house in Essex Road (on the right hand side some 250 metres past the end of Camden Passage), close to Cross Street, was often visited by Samuel Pepys, for he mentions in his diary that in 1664 his father used to carry the family to Islington, where they had cakes and ale at the Queens Head. The pub still exists, and still has a fine early fireplace on the first floor.

During the 1500 & 1600s, Islington was a keen archery centre. The famous Dame Alice Owen's School was

128

The Old Queens Head public house in Georgian times. It has since been rebuilt but it has retained a magnificent very early fireplace. Highly recommended for a visit, a drink and a viewing, just a couple of hundred metres along the Essex Road.

founded just behind the Angel, between Goswell Road and St John's Street, in 1623. The story goes that Dame Alice Owen was walking in the meadows when an arrow pierced the high-domed hat that she was wearing and, to thank God for her lucky escape, she vowed to found a school on the very spot. This she did, and I thank her for it, as that is where I was educated. Owen's School is famous, amongst other attributes, for handing out 'Beer Money' to its students once a year – in place of the ale which the patrons, the Brewers Guild, used to dole out to them. The school building is still there, although the school was moved out for safety during the second world war, and has never returned.

The soil of a great part of Islington was highly suitable for the making of bricks, so that a brick factory flourished from as far back as 1580, and became more and more busy as the

129

demand for houses to be built in Islington increased. It seems that the brick factory workers attracted some of the less desirable types, the Recorder of London in the late sixteenth century noting that 'the Savoy and brick kilns near Islington' brought forth rogues and vagabonds.

The late seventeenth and early eighteenth century saw many pubs and teahouses spring up around the Angel and Islington Green. The Angel was an important coaching station, with mail and passenger coaches resting their horses and passengers in the local hostelry before proceeding to the City or heading for the North.

As Islington was a place where drovers spent the night, having shepherded their flock into pens which were part of the local business, there were some cheap and, by all accounts, pretty bawdy establishments to cater for them. In fact, the night life of Islington was quite an attraction to many inhabitants of the City of London, who had merely to travel along City Road and up the hill to the Angel (risking being robbed by the numerous highwaymen working that beat) to be in the thick of it. Bull-baiting, duck hunting, equestrian events and bare-fist prize-fighting were some of the varied attractions, and one cannot help wondering where 'The Bailiff's Daughter of Islington' of the well-known ballad, came into the scene. At the other end of the scale, Sadlers Wells was there for the cultured – coming from the City, just turn *left* at the Angel, along St John's Street and turn right into Theobald Road.

By the latter part of the eighteenth and well into the nineteenth century, Islington had blossomed into a great entertainment venue, tea-houses providing additional attractions such as concerts and balloon ascents, and we can see why shopfronts were added to the High Street houses, and The Gun pub at 106 High Street flourished. It is also easy to understand why Londoners began to see the benefit of living in this country area where the air was cleaner. Rich merchants built houses to suit their status, with quarters for the servants, such as can be seen in Duncan Terrace, Colebrooke Row, Canonbury and, even larger, in Highbury New Park. It is in one of these houses in Highbury New Park that Cecil Rhodes lived. The Rhodes family had a long connection with Islington, for Cecil's

Islington in 1780
Camden Passage on right.

Reproduced by kind permission of Islington Library.

grandfather purchased the dairy farm owned by Mr Pullin (Pullins Row – 90–98 High Street) in the early nineteenth century. Rhodes and a Mr Charles Laycock were the two largest dairy farmers in the area, on whom much of the City relied for milk and butter. Laycock was also the largest goose and poultry feeder in England prior to his son building up the dairy interest. It was these two dairy farmers who were responsible for the many hundreds of milkmaids who walked out from the City, milked the cows into their pails and then walked back to sell their milk door to door to the populace of London, their pails supported by wooden yolks across their shoulders.

These farmers also rented out enclosures where the drovers, on their way with their flocks of sheep or cattle to Smithfield Meat Market (still there and worth a visit while inspecting St Bartholomew's Church), rested for the night. If one looks at how Upper Street (the road from the north) and Essex Road (the road from the east) merge at Islington

Charles Dickens visited Caroline Chisholm in this house
in Charlton Place.

Green, it can be seen how important an area for such an enterprise the Angel was. In fact, so much traffic of animals was taking place that the residents complained loudly enough for an Act of Parliament to be enacted, which forbade the movement of animals through the Parish during the hours of Divine Service.

The population of Islington multiplied rapidly during the 1800s, rising from 10,000 in that year to 335,000 in 1900, the years 1840 – 1880 seeing the most rapid expansion. It is now only 160,000.

A WALK OF SOME HISTORICAL INTEREST

Starting at the intersection of Camden Passage and Charlton Place, walking down the hill, we very quickly arrive at No.32 Charlton Place, on the wall of which is a blue plaque which states that Caroline Chisholm, 1808–1877, lived here. At the time she lived there, it was No.3 Charlton Crescent, and she is shown in the 1852 Islington Directory as 'Mrs Chisholm, Family Colonisation Loan Society'. The plaque describes her as 'Philanthropist. The Emigrants' Friend.'

Caroline Chisholm was some sort of saint, and there was in fact a proposal to make her one. Certainly the Australian government holds her in sufficient esteem to put her portrait on the five-dollar notes. She set out to raise funds to aid girls who were sent to the colonies, particularly to Australia, where they were met by a motley variety of men loitering at the docks, waiting to see what they could pick up. Caroline would escort the girls from the moment of disembarkation, and help them run the gauntlet of city-slickers. She would ride with the young girls to the outback farms to secure them employment. When she returned to England, she took up residence in Charlton Crescent where she singlehandedly organized her Society in order to help people get out to Australia. Millions of today's Australians owe their nationality to the purposefulness of this determined lady.

There were few celebrities who were not approached by Caroline, asking for funds and also for them to help publicise her campaign. An appeal to Charles Dickens

Colebrooke Cottage
LAMB'S HOUSE
AT ISLINGTON

To F. V. HALLAM
from J. T. C. WEEKS

(From a Contemporary Drawing.)

134

Charles Lamb's House.
Duncan Terrace,
Islington.

resulted in that great gentleman arriving at No.3 Charlton Crescent. From what I can understand, Dickens was a bit of a pompous, self-important man, and it came as an annoyance to him to have his deliberations constantly interrupted by Caroline's children thumping up and down the carpeted stairs. It is not recorded whether he did help the cause but, with a little imagination, one can see him arriving along the cobbled road in a hansom cab.

Our next port of call takes us to the bottom of Charlton Place, and a right turn takes us along Colebrooke Row. The third turning to the left is Noel Road. Here, from 1959, lived Joe Orton, the playwright, author of *Entertaining Mr Sloane* and *Loot*. Joe made an ignoble exit from Noel Road after he was beaten to death by his male lover, who then took an overdose of drugs to join him. There is an official commemorative plaque on the house but as it is on the wall outside his flat and that flat was on the top floor, it is better visible to the occupants of the houses opposite and then only if they look out of their top floor windows!

Let us walk back up Noel Road, turn left at the top and take a look at the Regents Canal which was opened in 1820. There is a most pleasant walk to be had along the footpath, reached by stairs from Colebrooke Row. This is the scene of artist Sickert's 'Hanging Gardens of Islington'. Up to the late 1930s, this canal was still used for its original purpose, although it was nowhere near as busy as it was in the nineteenth century – to transport merchandise from Paddingon to the Limehouse docks. The bargees lay on their backs and 'footed it' along the roof of the tunnel to propel their barges, hence the expression. Once out of the tunnel, a cart-horse was hitched up for the rest of the journey.

If we now return to Colebrooke Row and retrace our steps past the bottom of Charlton Place, we arrive at Lamb's Cottage as it is known but more correctly, Colebrooke Cottage, on your left. The poet Charles Lamb, his wife and adopted daughter, lived their romantic and dramatic lives there in the 1820s. At that time, the house was larger than it now is, and the New River was running outside their front door and Islington was decidedly rural. The New River is still there, but has been covered in for many years.

There are some fine houses in Colebrooke Row and Duncan Terrace, and an idea of the life that existed there in the late nineteenth century was provided in 1963 by Camden Passage's then oldest inhabitant.

Until 1963, 102 Islington High Street was occupied by Allans – 'the oil shop'. Here you could buy oil lamps, oil heaters, gas mantles and supplies of paraffin oil. Surprisingly, there was still a brisk trade in oil lamps, and the theory was that tenants in the shared houses suspected that their co-tenants were using more electricity than they (they were on a shared cost basis), and therefore preferred to use oil lamps. Mr Stephens was the proprietor ever since I could remember, and a dear, polite and courteous little man he was. In 1963, he had reached the age of 93 and was still serving in the shop in his habitual deferential manner, helped by his son. He told me that in 1855 he had made his way, mainly walking, to London from a small village in Wales, and on arrival in London he got a menial boy's job at the oil shop owned by Mr Allan. When Mr Allan eventually died, he inherited the shop.

'There were grand people living in those big houses in Duncan Terrace when I came to London,' he reminisced. 'They would have their carriages draw up, and out would come the ladies in their finery. They might be going to Sadlers Wells or a theatre in London or to Highgate Hill, or for a picnic on Hampstead Heath. That lasted for many years, until it became more fashionable to live further out in the suburbs. The whole of Islington was fashionable in those days – not like it is now.' He did not live to see Islington return to being the fashionable place that it has again become.

There are many places to visit in Islington – Canonbury Square, Sadlers Wells, Chapel Market, Agricultural Hall – but we are staying close to Camden Passage, which has seen Islington in its bawdy days, then the more elegant Victorian and Edwardian era; back to a run-down suburb, and now 'the' place to live.

137

Above: Canonbury Tower.

Below: Chapel Street Market.

These delightful drawings by 'Geordie', Bill Crawford show his love for Islington and his meticulous style.

Above: The Catholic Church of St John the Evangelist.

Below: The famous Collin's Music Hall.

139

13

Just before I left Camden Passage to go to live in Australia in 1969, I took Asher Oldschool to an old burnt-out warehouse situated at the point where Camden Passage ends and Islington Green starts. Mr Oldschool had been taking quite an interest in Camden Passage, and I knew he had clients who would be interested in investing in the area.

'Turn the groundfloor into a Georgian Village with all the shops with replicas of early Georgian shopfronts. A restaurant upstairs and perhaps some offices, and you should have a success on your hands.'

In the event, he did a lot more than I ever envisaged, turning the upper floors into high-class offices and attracting very good tenants. The Georgian Village is charming, and there are shops on the first floor and in the basement. I know Mr Oldschool, who took on the project with a partner, did not have an easy time for quite a few years, but he certainly did his bit for Camden Passage. He was later, in the early 1970s, to buy 116 and 118 Islington High Street when Guy des Rochers retired from his Angel Antiques business. He has made another arcade of shops on the ground floor and basement, and has his offices above and very nice they are, too.

Some years before, in 1966, I had tried to interest one of Mr Oldschool's contacts in the old power station which stood in a complete block in front of Phelps Cottage. This had been the transformer station for the tramway system which was disbanded in the early 1950s, to be replaced by trolley-buses, which in turn were replaced by diesel buses. It gave off a constant high-pitched whistle, which those of us who have lived within earshot got so used to that we

140

never heard it. On occasions, we had relatives stay with us at 106 High Street, and gave them the top front bedroom. They reported that they could not sleep because of the noise. From then on, we gave them the back bedroom which faced onto the extensive gardens behind, and which were unbelievably quiet at night when one considers they were in the centre of London, except when a few tom-cats serenaded each other in preparation for a fight.

Mr Oldschool's client was quite interested in converting the power station, but the London Transport Board could not make a decision of any sort, and after a large pile of fruitless correspondence, he dropped out. There is now a fine conversion in the form of The Mall, which, although beautifully done, can tend to be claustrophobic. My original unadopted plan made use of the outside, so that the shops had plenty of daylight, one set facing to Upper Street and the others to High Street.

This story is about Camden Passage, but I am so often asked why I left England for Australia that I think I should explain. I was born in Camden Passage and spent my whole life there, apart from five war years in the army. Once I knew that Camden Passage would continue to grow and flourish, I thought that I should try to do something exciting. I had made myself the 'dogsbody' of The Passage for ten years, and needed a change. This was the era of Harold Wilson, and all the inflation and frustration that went with his brand of government. With two young sons to educate, it seemed to me that England was not the best place to be for their sakes. We went to Australia, thinking that if we did not like it we would go somewhere else or even return to England. When we arrived, we found Sydney to be a delightful place with a far better climate than England's. We stayed.

The title of this book is inspired by an album presented to me at a small ceremony before we left for Australia. It has a gold-blocked title – 'From Camden Passage With Love'. Organized by Victoria Davidson, artist, antique dealer and good friend, who was an enthusiastic collaborator from the moment she took a shop in Pierrepont Arcade in 1963. The album contains tributes and expressions of thanks from everyone connected with Camden Passage. It is a treasured possession. A cartoon from the album, drawn by Victoria, appears on page 114.

I had appointed John Friend, whose O'Hara's toy/cycle/pram shop had closed in favour of the rents the premises would bring if let to antique dealers, to be manager of the two arcades – Gateway and Pierrepont – and the stalls, a job which he kept and found exciting for twenty years up to his retirement. An Ansafone installed in our office in Phelps Cottage and another in my offices in Sydney proved to be the perfect way for me to maintain control of the everyday affairs of Camden Passage.

Thanks to the wonders of communication – the telephone, the answering machine and now the fax, and the Jumbo 747, which, thanks to Qantas or British Airways, I use to travel home once a year, I am never far away from Camden Passage, despite the 12,000 miles that separate us. I am also happy that I can keep a measure of control and influence over the affairs of Camden Passage so that it may remain a happy community and not be subject too much to the greed of dispassionate landlords.

Just a short time ago, I happened to be passing by the antique shop near Bondi Beach, of one Addie Fisher, an old friend. It was some twelve months since I had seen him, and I popped in for a chat. We were sitting and talking for some time when an electrician walked in, his tools about his waist in a leather satchel. After some chatting between them about the job Addie required done, he introduced him to me and said:

'He's a Pom, too.' (They talk like that!)

'How long have you been here?' I asked.

'Twenty years.'

'Same here. What part of London are you from?' – I had identified his accent.

'Islington,' he replied.

'Oh! So you would know Camden Passage?'

'Do you know the restaurants in Camden Passage?' he countered.

'Most certainly I do.'

'My brother was the first chef who worked at "Fredericks". He designed the kitchens. Pulman's his name. He lives out here now, semi-retired.'

'"Fredericks" was my home before I left Camden Passage!' I told him.

Nearly 20,000 kilometres (12,000 miles) from 'home'; a complete stranger; a chance meeting, and pinpointing the very place I sold to 'Fredericks'!